Before Ron Wal[illegible] nanage-ment consultant with a gove[illegible], he had never written any fiction stories. After finding [illegible]at he had much leisure time at a retirement home, he tried his hand at writing his first novel, entitled *The Mysteries of the Haunted Isle.*

He has now written this autobiography that records his life as a child in World War II from the ages of three to eight. It includes his vivid experiences during the London Blitz and raids by the V1s (flying bombs) and V2s (the first long-range ballistic missiles) – rockets that travelled several times faster than the speed of sound.

Ron J. Wallington

A Child at War

Austin Macauley Publishers®
London * Cambridge * New York * Sharjah

All of the events in this memoir are true to the best of author's memory. The views expressed in this memoir are solely those of the author.

A CIP catalogue record for this title is available from the British Library.

ISBN 9781035892266 (Paperback)
ISBN 9781035892273 (ePub e-book)

www.austinmacauley.com

First Published 2025
Austin Macauley Publishers Ltd®
1 Canada Square
Canary Wharf
London
E14 5AA

My name is Ron Wallington. I was born on Christmas Eve at Boundary Road, Chatham, Kent, in 1935, just over three years before the start of WW2. After my beloved wife died, I moved to a care home near Bristol. The home provided for all my needs and left me time to think about what to do with my spare time. My three teenage granddaughters once questioned me about what it was like to grow up in wartime. Their question provoked me to write this short autobiography. Most of my story is about my experiences that I can clearly remember, but I have also added some useful information that I have gleaned from various sources.

Boundary Road separated Chatham from the historic city of Rochester. It had a large Norman castle and a very beautiful cathedral, built in 654 AD. It is the second oldest cathedral in England. In 1078, Gundulf, Bishop of Rochester, founded St. Bartholomew's Hospital for lepers on the outskirts of Rochester. The author, Charles Dickens, spent many years of his early life in the city. Several sites, such as The Old Curiosity Shop and the seven children's graves from Great Expectations, appear in his novels. It was also the home of Short's, the seaplane manufacturers. Often, their small seaplanes could be seen in the River Medway in Rochester. Mum told me that Chatham, too, was a very famous town. It had a large naval port and a very illustrious history as a dockyard. It had been building ships since the 1560s. It was the major port involved in the three Anglo-Dutch Wars (whatever they were). The most famous battleship that they had ever built and repaired there was Lord Nelson's ship, the Victory. They were now building submarines for the Royal Navy. Chatham was also the home base of the Royal Marines for many centuries until 1948, when they moved to Deal.

Mum and I moved to a very nice rented house in Simonds Avenue, Chatham. Dad did not live with us at the time as he was serving in the Royal Navy away at sea, where he was soon to complete a 12-year employment contract. In 1938, I was too young to know about what was happening in the world, but in later years my schoolmasters taught me the vital history of WW2. In 1938, British and French secret agents reported to London and Paris that Germany was rearming and preparing to invade and conquer European countries. Hitler had already seized the former German-speaking port of Danzig in Poland and was about to occupy the Sudetenland, a former German province in Czechoslovakia. Hitler, the German leader, said the nation needed 'room to breathe.' The concept of 'Lebensraum' had been common in Germanic politics since 1890. The British government did not fully trust Hitler and began to take steps to protect the population in the event of war. The first step taken was to issue gas masks to everyone. Every day at school, we would practice putting on our gas masks that we carried in a small cardboard box everywhere we went. There were special masks for babies in prams or cots and some Mickey Mouse-style masks for young children. We schoolchildren were given full-sized masks. They looked very frightening to us, and we did not like putting them on. The first use of modern-style gas warfare was by the

Germans at the Battle of Ypres in 1915. Many thousands of British and colonial soldiers died until the Germans ceased using the gas weapon for fear of retaliation from the Allies. Gas, perhaps by agreement, was not used in WW2, and we were informed that there was no longer any need to carry our little brown boxes around with us.

Despite the peace talks that were proceeding between Britain and Germany, the UK government felt the need to evacuate children to the safety of the countryside in case the enemy decided to attack our ports and other strategic targets. In 1938, the government set up 'Operation Pied Piper' and evacuated nearly a million children to the care of families in safer parts of England who would willingly accept them. Before the children boarded their trains, they had labels pinned on their clothing to identify who they were and the family they were going to. In the section following, you will find a section of an essay written by a schoolboy, Stanley Lodder, in October 1938. The original can be seen in the Museum of London. He writes about what was happening in UK schools before Britain declared war on Germany.

On Monday, the order came through that all families were to go to Turnham Road School and be fitted with gas masks. My friend, Donald Broom-Smith, and I were the first ones in our respective families to see this notice, so at the first possible moment, we told our mothers about it. On Monday evening, we all went down to the school and were fitted for our masks. On Tuesday morning, Mr Green said, "Owing to the Council's evacuation scheme, all boys who live over twenty minutes' walk away from this school and who are coming must bring their luggage on Wednesday morning." As soon as I got home, I told my mother about the developments. At once, she packed a suitcase full of clothes and a satchel full of food. On Wednesday, I brought my luggage to school and put it in the classroom. Gradually, the situation got worse and worse. At four o'clock, the situation took a turn for the better, and on Friday, our Prime Minister, Neville Chamberlain, announced that Hitler, Mussolini, and Daladier had arranged a peace pact. Mr Green told us to take our luggage home. I am very glad that there was no bloodshed and slaughter in Europe.

When Neville Chamberlain arrived back at Heston Airport, he proudly displayed the 'piece of paper' which today is believed to be a peace agreement between Britain, France, and Germany. Several weeks after the peace talks had ended, Germany invaded Poland. Britain and France had a peace treaty with Poland in which they pledged to assist the country if it were threatened. In retaliation for the invasion, Britain and France declared war on Germany on 3rd September 1939. It is reported that the UK population had no great love for Poland, with its unpopular and corrupt dictatorship. Many of the leaders in British industry favoured the Nazis because they imprisoned Trade Union members and persecuted the Jews. Even the British short-reigned King, Edward, visited Hitler and was warmly welcomed. Neville Chamberlain and many members of his party were in Favor of the peace treaty with Germany, but Winston Churchill, the next Prime Minister, was strongly against this as he did not trust the old enemy from WWI. On 3rd September 1939, Britain and France declared war on Germany. Once the war started, the Navy's task was to protect all the cargo ships bringing food and goods from America and elsewhere to Britain. Their enemy was the large packs of German submarines (Unterwasser boats). Their task was to torpedo our ships and stop their cargo from getting to Britain. Hitler reckoned that if we could not get any supplies, we would have to surrender, and the Germans would make us all slaves. The enemy sank over 4,000 ships and killed over 72,000 crewmen before they were defeated. Dad came home on embarkation leave at Christmas. He had been on duty with the Royal Navy in the Atlantic protecting our convoys. He had also just come back from the USA after his ship had carried King George IV and Queen Elizabeth on a visit to America. He had made some good friends there, and every Christmas, they sent me a five-dollar note. At Christmas 1942, they had sent me a hamper with some toys in it, but the ship carrying it was torpedoed, and so I never saw my present! I don't remember meeting Dad until I was about three years old. Before then, I guess I was too young to remember him. It was not uncommon for sailors in the Royal Navy to be posted away from home for long periods of time. Before he met Mum, he had once been based in Shanghai, China, for two and a half years. Soldiers serving in some countries in the war were also away from home for long periods, and some of my new school friends only had photos of their fathers to remember them by. We, too, had a framed photograph of Dad fastened to our living room wall. As I mentioned earlier, on the 3rd of September, 1939, Britain and France declared war on Germany. Mum told me later that day that as I was sitting at a table looking at some picture books, it was getting a little dark, so I got up and scrambled on a chair to reach the room light. "Don't put the light on," screamed my mother as I reached up to touch the switch. "The Germans might see the light and drop a bomb on us!" I did not even know who or what the Germans were or why they should want to drop a bomb on us. What was a bomb anyway? Mum tried to explain it all to me. A few days later, I was playing in our back garden with my young friend Eddie when a single-engine aircraft (probably a famous Messerschmitt BF109) flew overhead and circled around.

I remember that I was terrified and ran indoors and screamed to Mum, "There's an aeroplane in the sky above us! Is it going to drop a bomb on us?" Mum went out to look.

She came back and said, "I have seen it. Don't worry, it is probably only a German spy-plane looking for the Dockyard. I expect he will fly away in a moment and will not drop a bomb on us." That is just what it did. Some days later, a German bomber did drop a landmine on Chatham Dockyard. At the beginning of the war, Mum and I were given Identity Cards. Mum got a green one, and I got a brown one. Mum said we were to keep them on us at all times in case we were asked to prove our identity. I was only asked for one once. I was only about four years old, and I decided that I would go alone and visit my grandparents living in London.

When I got to the station, the ticket office clerk looked at me incredulously and said, "Show me your Identity Card." Of course I did not have one with me, and I went home disappointed. I did not consider what the reaction my Mum would have had if I had not returned home! We were never asked to show them to anybody afterwards, and they were withdrawn at the end of the war. The blackout regulations were soon to come into force in January 1940. Air Raid Wardens (like the one portrayed in the BBC series *Dad's Army* would patrol the streets at night and shout, "Put that light out!"

if any householder had any light showing. Mum put up some blackout curtains and spread some brown sticky tape across the windows. I told Mum that I did not think the tape would stop much light escaping. She explained that if a bomb exploded near us, the 'wind' from the explosion might damage the glass in the windows, and the brown tape might stop them from breaking. One event that I did notice was that the street lamplighter had stopped coming with his calcium carbide rod to ignite the roadside gas lamps outside our houses and so left our street in darkness.

All motor vehicles had their headlamps shielded to help prevent any unnecessary light from showing to low-flying bombers. Some say that even the light from cigarettes could be seen by low-flying bombers. When Dad came home on leave at Christmas 1939, we told him that a landmine had been dropped on Chatham Dockyard. He was alarmed and advised us to move from our home and find somewhere safe to live, perhaps with my grandparents in Brixton, London. 'Hitler will only want to attack military targets like Chatham Dockyard, so he won't bomb London,' he confidently predicted. He was partly right. I learned at school that during the war, many children (about a million) were evacuated to safe homes, usually in the countryside and on farms. After the war, the evacuees were expected to return home, but some parents did not care to receive them. They may not have seen them for five years and perhaps did not like the expense of bringing them up. Some children did not want to go home and leave their country paradise! At Christmas 1939, we travelled by Greenline coach up to Gran and Grandad's house in Brixton, London. While we were there, Dad suggested that it might be a good idea for Mum and me to move to a safe place near them, as Hitler only wanted to bomb airfields and not cities. They were very pleased with the idea and promised to help find us a suitable house near them. When Dad's leave had ended, he was posted from the Atlantic to join the fleet in the Mediterranean. The day before he left us, it was snowing hard, and Dad took me into the back garden and helped me build a snowman. It was the first time that I can remember Dad had played with me. When Dad set off to join the fleet, he kissed Mum 'Goodbye' and gave me a big hug. I did not know then that Mum was very worried that this might be the last time they saw each other, as the death rate in the Mediterranean was high. Regretfully, many thousands of British seamen did not return home. Gran and Grandad were very pleased to help us and soon found us a small terraced house near them. When we saw it and moved in, I was very disappointed. It was in a very scruffy condition, not like our old home. It had no electricity, no indoor toilet, nor a bathroom. The only light source when it got dark was the two gas lamps over the mantelpiece. In order to light them, you had first to turn on the gas supply to them and then apply a lighted match to a small gas mantel. Mum soon arranged for electricity to be connected. We were the first in the street to do so. The house had a small living room, a very small kitchen, and a scullery that contained a brick-built boiler, containing a large metal basin to do the washing in, an old gas cooker, a heavy clothes mangle, and a small sink. The boiler had a small fire grate underneath to boil the water for washing the dishes and for washing clothes, as well as to supply water for our weekly bath. I remember when I needed my bath, we had to unhook a large tin bath off the wall in the garden, then place it by the lit fire in the living room and fill it with hot water from the clothes boiler. After the bath, we emptied the water by the bucketful down the drain in the back garden and then hung the bath back on the kitchen wall to dry. The outside toilet at the end of the house in the back garden had no gas lamp or electric light, and on winter nights, it was a nightmare to leave our warm house and plod through the rain or snow to the freezing cold toilet. In those days, toilet paper was a luxury, and we had to make use of newspaper cut up into squares and hung on a hook in a space in the corner of the room. We had only a very small back garden and only a very tiny front one. The main source of heating and some cooking was a Kitchener fireplace and oven in the living room. This consisted of a place in the middle of the oven to build a fire, with a small oven on the side. When the fire was lit and burning bright, the oven would get very hot and was often used to cook meals in. On top of the oven were flat surfaces on which you could put pots to boil water or cook vegetables. There was a place at the rear of the oven top—the back burner—where we would leave a large pot filled with water to heat for any future use. The fire heated the room too, and you could make toast by holding a slice of bread on a toasting fork in front of the fire section. Often, we had used up our ration of butter or margarine and could only spread some cooking lard or jam straight onto the bread. The jam was partly made with sawdust to give it bulk. I was very unhappy about the move at first, but once I had made some friends at school, I soon forgot about the problems of our new home. Perhaps one of the first effects of the declaration of war was the introduction of food rationing in January 1940. I did not know it at the time, but most of our food was imported from abroad, and the Germans had organised packs of submarines to torpedo ships carrying food to Britain. The enemy hoped we would surrender once the food had run out. Every man, woman, and child was given a ration book: a beige-coloured one for adults and a green one for children. It contained details of the amount of various foods that you were entitled to purchase, if they were available, such as bread, butter, margarine, meat, eggs, cheese, confectionery, etc. You had to register with the stores where you were going to get your rations. Some food items were off the ration, such as rabbits and broken biscuits. I remember the Woolworth's store in Brixton selling broken biscuits at three pence per bag. The Ministry of Food encouraged everyone to supplement their diets by growing fruit and vegetables in their gardens or allotments. They called it the "Dig for Victory" campaign and had posters printed and displayed in public places. Many lawns and green areas in public places were dug up and vegetables planted in their place. Eggs were rationed too, at one egg per person per week. Children could have two. Grandad suggested that Mum and I try keeping a few chickens to supplement our egg supply. He came and built us a little hen house and fenced off a small area for the birds to exercise. He then obtained about five hens for us. It worked very well, and I'll always remember the thrill of going to the hen house and finding a newly laid egg in the straw. If you had very many chickens, you were required to give your surplus supply of eggs to the government. The government once experimented with using whale meat, but it was not universally liked. "It's like eating steak with cod liver oil," said one person.

"It tastes very fishy," said another, and the idea was soon abandoned. The very first item to be rationed was petrol. This did not directly worry us, as few working-class families owned a motor vehicle. Only the doctor, headmaster, and bank manager had cars. Bread, milk, groceries, fish, and even coal all came by horse and cart. The local corner shop and the greengrocer could supply needed food if you were registered with them. Recycling was not a new idea. There were at least two men with horses and carts who regularly visited our streets in search of used or scrap materials. The first was a man who came shouting, "Rag and Bone! Rag and Bone!" What became of the rag and bone that he collected, I wonder?

A second man also came around regularly shouting, "Any old iron, any old iron." Already the government had passed legislation allowing them to cut down iron fences, gates, etc., and use the haul to produce weapons of war. A third campaigner for recycling was Lord Beaverbrook—a newspaper magnate—who urged housewives to donate any surplus aluminium pots and pans 'to help produce Spitfires'. Unfortunately, the collected aluminium was not the right type to make aircraft! What worried us most was the rationing of coal. Coal was needed not only for heating the house but for boiling water and cooking on the Kitchener stove that was fitted in most small houses. We were allowed just two hundredweight of coal a week. This was hardly enough, and we had to supplement the supply with wood when we could find some. Our coal storage place was in a large cupboard in the space in the living room under the stairs! Some neighbours stored their supply outside in the back garden. When the USA entered the war, we began to receive some supplies from them as the German submarine force was curtailed. Perhaps the USA food item that I remember most was the cardboard cartons of dried egg. Imaginative cooks could do a lot with them, but not everyone liked them. Clothes rationing was introduced in June 1941. School-aged children were given extra coupons to help them buy school uniforms. The Ministry of Food realised that children needed to supplement their limited diet and introduced bottles of orange juice and cod liver oil. The cod liver oil was disliked and was later replaced with Virol, a popular spreadable malt extract. Food rationing did not stop until 1954; the last food on ration was meat. The National Health Service had not yet been set up until 1948, so we had to rely on the local doctor to deal with our health problems. I believe that we paid about three shillings each time we visited him or her, but I am not sure. When we could, we relied on home remedies to satisfy our needs. The most common treatment for small wounds and scrapes was a coating of iodine on the wound. It seemed to work. Another popular medicine was 'paregoric.' It was made from a form of opium and was used to alleviate stomach aches and a multitude of other ailments. In winter, Mum used to put a layer of 'thermogene wool' on my chest. This was a medicated wadding that was given to relieve rheumatism, lumbago, bronchitis, sciatica, chest colds, sore throats, neuralgia, neuritis, and a host of other conditions. And of course, you always had Aspro for all kinds of pain. You could be sent to the local hospital for serious illnesses. Our sources of entertainment were often the cinema, the radio, or card or board games with friends or neighbours. Often we would stroll over to Gran and Grandad's and play 'shove-ha'penny' or dominoes. We borrowed a rare copy of Monopoly from a neighbour, and after the war was over, Dad came home and made a playable copy of it on top of the steel Morrison shelter that had been installed. We made imitation money and some cardboard houses. Cinemas were ordered to close at the beginning of the war but were allowed to reopen after just a week to boost morale. Mum used to take me to the cinema once a week with our usual ration of acid drops to chew as we watched the films. Usually, they were adult films, but sometimes they might be a Disney epic or my favourite—a Western—with Roy Rogers or Gene Autry. My favourite radio programme for children was Children's Hour at 5 o'clock every weekday evening. The host was 'Uncle Mac'. In the evenings, we often listened to shows like ITMA with Tommy Handley or music programmes with Vera Lynn or Donald Peers. Paul Temple, the private detective series, was another favourite. Other favourite programmes—mainly for adults—were *Music While You Work* and *Workers' Playtime*. Whenever Dad was home, he used to read to us. Our choice at the weekend used to be *Saturday Night Theatre*, read by the American actress Gladys Cooper. My reading as a small boy was the Dandy and the Beano. As I got older, I used to make good use of the public libraries. The newspapers had very few pages as there was a need to save paper. Sundays were a biblical day of rest. Only essential people were allowed to go to work. Sunday was a very quiet day. No one kicked cans up the street on Sunday! Cinemas and theatres were closed, as were all places of entertainment. All the shops were closed, and the only places to go to meet other people were the churches and chapels. I believe public houses were still open. For many, it was church and Sunday School in the morning and perhaps a quiet walk in the afternoon. Not long after we moved to London, the authorities began to build air-raid shelters to protect us in the possible event of any attacks by the Luftwaffe. There were three types of shelter. The first was a public shelter, built of brick, for anyone caught outside during an air raid. It was not popular as it was often used as a public toilet and smelled strongly of urine. The second type was the popular Anderson shelter. It was made of six curved pieces of special steel that were bolted together and sunk 3 feet into the ground and covered with earth. People with large savings or high incomes could buy one for £7, but the average householder obtained one free. It would be a very safe place to shelter unless it was struck by a direct hit. It was planned to accommodate six people, but my grandparents often had some frightened neighbours come and join them during an air raid. Some keen homeowners would try to make the shelter more like home by decorating it, both inside and out. The third shelter was the Morrison shelter. This was supplied to people who did not have space in their garden to erect a shelter. This was the type Mum and I used to shelter in if we did not have time to run to our grandparents' Anderson shelter. It consisted of a large steel table with strong wire netting around the sides to prevent any fallen debris from hitting them. The Germans did not bomb London at first, as Dad had prophesied. I am told that their initial targets were RAF airfields and aircraft. They believed that once these were put out of action, they would be able to launch a sea invasion of Britain. They had a plan entitled "Adlertag" or "Eagle Day" in which they would attempt to destroy the RAF by attacking and making their airfields unserviceable. The raids started on August 13th, 1940. The first one to be attacked and destroyed was Manston in Kent. The enemy attacked with a squadron of Messerschmitt BF110 bombers. Luckily, all but one of the 29 Hurricanes and Spitfires took off in time to avoid the attack. The German attacks on our airfields were going well until the

Luftwaffe accidentally dropped some bombs on London—it seems by mistake! In retaliation, the RAF made a raid on Berlin. The German people were shocked that this could happen to them. Hitler was furious. Although little lasting damage was done by the raid, he screamed, "For every bomb they drop on Germany, I will repay them a hundredfold!" He then cancelled the raids on airfields and directed his aircraft to bomb the cities. Some historians write that it was just what Churchill had wanted to prevent the airfields from being destroyed. We had been living safely in London until September 1940 when the Blitz commenced; then we experienced raids every night and some during the day. The Blitz ended in May 1941. Over 43,000 Londoners were killed and more than 50,000 injured. We found safety in Gran's shelter, but life was not very pleasant. It was cramped, damp, and rather smelly, especially when the solitary oil lamp was burning. As a young child, I was given the privilege of sleeping on the only bunk on one side of the shelter. I forget how the others rested. Sometimes Gran would bring in cut sandwiches that she had made earlier. We did not have refrigerators in those days, so Gran had to keep them fresh by wrapping them in newspaper. If we desperately needed a toilet, we might chance our luck and make a quick dash for the outside toilet in between the air raids. I am told that some families kept a bucket for use in emergencies. We had to rely on an old oil lamp for our only means of light, and this made it difficult to read a newspaper or a book. Nevertheless, I remember one neighbour trying to knit some garment in the poor light. We must have had a small table because I can remember us all playing cards on it. Our small radio did not work in our shelter. We often stayed there all night until the welcome single-note 'All Clear' siren sounded. The Battle of Britain was going on above us, and we could hear the Hurricanes and Spitfires overhead as they attacked the Dornier and Heinkel bombers and their Messerschmitt fighter escorts. Thanks to the British and Polish airmen, the Germans lost so many aircraft that Hitler cancelled the raids and turned his attention to the Russian enemy in the East. In the early period of the war, the Hurricane fighter was our main fighter aircraft and concentrated on attacking enemy bombers, while the later well-known Spitfire successfully concentrated on attacking the escort fighters. Our Prime Minister, Winston, often broadcast rousing speeches to boost morale and keep us looking forward to a victorious future. In one of his broadcasts, he praised the actions of our Battle of Britain pilots with the famous phrase, *"Never, in the field of human conflict, has so much been owed by so many to so few."* Our teacher informed me that it was thought that Hitler's attacks on cities and towns in Britain were his greatest mistake in the war. It is said that the Luftwaffe should have been used to bomb more important targets elsewhere. The German fighters protecting the bombers from the Allied fighters had only fuel for ten minutes over Britain before they had to turn back. The result was that their bombers suffered high casualties and found that attacking London and elsewhere was very costly in aircrews and aircraft. The air raids were very terrifying for both adults and children. I can remember sitting in the shelter, listening to the whistling sound of bombs crashing down on us and the resulting explosions as they destroyed our homes and factories. Grandad spoke to me to try to allay my fears: 'If you can hear them whistling down, you will know it is not for you!' One night after an air raid, I walked to school in the morning to discover a stick of nine bombs had destroyed a row of houses and a pub (the Monty) in my street, not 100 yards from our house, killing several adults and children. On another occasion, Mum and I left Gran's shelter, where we had spent the night, and as we approached our house, we found the road barricaded off and ARP officers preventing access to our house. We could see a very large crater right in front of our home, knocking down our small garden wall. The ARP informed us that a 500-pound time bomb had fallen in front of our house and that we could not go in until the Bomb Disposal Team had defused it. When we eventually got access, we found that the shock of the falling bomb had brought down part of the ceiling in my bedroom! It was fortunate that it was a time bomb; else, it would have left us homeless! The air raids were usually, but not always, at night, and sometimes we would ignore the safety of the shelter and stand in the cover of the front doorway, watching the searchlights pick out and follow the German bombers in the night sky. In the morning, we lads would go around the streets collecting pieces of shrapnel named after the British army officer who invented it. The shrapnel came from the Bofors anti-aircraft shells and/or pieces of aircraft (German and British). We children would keep the pieces as souvenirs or swap them with friends for other goodies, such as marbles or cigarette cards. A burnt-out incendiary bomb – about the size of a litre canister of milk – was considered a very valuable find. The Luftwaffe found the incendiaries to be a very economical weapon. Instead of flying squadrons of heavy bombers to attack a target, it could send just three planes to scatter about 1,500 incendiary bombs over the selected area. The bombs, although small, could cause considerable damage. If one landed on your roof and rolled into the gutter, the magnesium content would explode and cause a fire that might burn your house down. The RAF considered them the most powerful weapon in the war. Apart from the damage to your property, some of the Fire Brigades might be pulled away from major fires to deal with the widespread domestic burning house crisis. The major defence against the incendiary bombs was the locally recruited Fire Guards, both men and women. My grandfather was one of the volunteers. His role was to stay awake during an air raid and spot and report any new fires. He was also equipped with a stirrup pump, with which he was expected to tackle any local blazes. The pump, once connected to a water supply, could be activated like a bicycle tire pump. The cylinder of water would be stood upright on the ground and secured firmly with both feet on the two stirrups at the bottom. By using a handle connected to a piece of apparatus inside the cylinder, the Fire Guard could pump a stream of water over a distance of 30 feet. My grandfather never had any occasion to make use of it, although it is recorded that 21 bombs fell in the Brixton Hill area. Air raids could be a very fearful time for us youngsters. If an air raid occurred while we were at school, we would march in an orderly manner to the school cellars until an air raid siren sounded the very welcome and continuous "All Clear." After the Blitz was thought to be over, we children came out of the shelters and started to enjoy the fresh air. We started to play games in the open again. Most of the games we play today, but some died away and new ones have taken their place. The boys had great fun playing Hide and Seek in any bombed houses. I can remember walking gingerly on exposed rafters or swinging across rooms on the exposed gas pipes. The girls liked skipping. They might stand on opposite sides of the traffic-free streets and pass a long skipping rope across the gap and then swing it. Several girls could then join in together. The boys and girls would also swing apart using smaller skipping ropes. Another favourite girls' game was with a wooden hoop and a stick, rolling it up and down the street. There were no plastic hula-hoops in those days. Perhaps the games the girls liked most were Hopscotch and drawing with chalk on the pavement, much to the annoyance of some tenants who rushed to pour water on their handiwork! Boys would gather 'conkers' where possible and have contests with other boys. Both girls and boys often played with cigarette cards, flicking them against a wall to gain points. Rolling marbles to get closest to a set marble (like in lawn bowls) was another great game. We played many games with a bat and ball. The bats were sometimes just pieces of wood, and the only balls we had were old tennis balls. The modern bladder-less footballs were not invented until after the war. We often played a form of cricket; the bails and wicket were chalked on any convenient wall. We also played French cricket, tennis, or rounders, or chase games like 'he' or 'it'. While we played, we had our ears open for the sound of any air-raid warning sirens, which would send us scurrying home to our shelters. Once the 'All Clear' had sounded, we would be out in the street again, perhaps searching for the expected shrapnel. If you were lucky enough to own a bicycle, you might risk a short ride about, but again you also had to listen carefully for any air-raid sirens. One game that I have not seen recently was *Knockdown Ginger*. It was a game played only by daring boys who wanted to impress the girls. The chosen boy had to knock on the front door of a house and run away and hide before the occupant opened it. The 'victim' was usually very annoyed. If we had to stay indoors, we would play simple card games, dominoes, Ludo, Snakes and Ladders, Noughts and Crosses, or play with our train sets if we were lucky. The girls had their dolls. Toys for both girls and boys were getting harder to buy as the factories making them now concentrated on producing items for the war. As we got older, we played more sophisticated games, such as chess, draughts, or backgammon, depending on what we could find in our toy cupboards. Eventually, we graduated to the most difficult and exciting board game of all – Monopoly. We played on Dad's home-made board on top of our Morrison indoor shelter, as explained earlier. Death was never far away. People were being killed in air raids. Pilots and crews of the Lancaster and other bombers that attacked targets in Germany and elsewhere had a very short life expectancy; fighter pilots were lucky to survive six weeks in action, soldiers were being killed every day, and sailors constantly risked being torpedoed or striking mines. But somehow, we never thought it might happen to us or our close friends. John Beard, our nineteen-year-old neighbour, was a night-fighter pilot. He was my personal hero, and he used to give me his cigarette cards that he collected from fellow pilots. He also had a pre-war Hornby train set that he used to show me occasionally. Despite our large age difference, we were great friends. One day, I asked him how he saw enemy aircraft in the dark. He replied, "Carrots. We pilots eat a lot of carrots. They help us to see better in the dark." I did not know then if he was just joking. I learned many years later that the Ministry ordered pilots to tell anyone interested that eating carrots was the reason for their good night vision. The idea of telling the story was to convince the Germans that eating carrots was the reason for their good sight and not some secret radar invention! In fact, we were using such a secret weapon very successfully. One morning after breakfast, John's mother knocked at the door. We could see she was very distressed. Her beloved son and my hero friend had been shot down and killed in the night. I had never felt so much grief in all my life, and it was a long time before I got over it. Fortunately, Dad was safe with the fleet in the Mediterranean, away from all the bombing. One evening at home, there was a rapid knock on our front door.

"I'll go," I said to Mum, "it will probably be my friends calling." It wasn't; it was my granddad.

"Mum in, I want to speak to her."

"What is it, Dad? Has Gran sent you for another cup of sugar?" said Mum.

He said, "No, guess you haven't heard the six o'clock news. It's about Dad's ship. It's been torpedoed off the coast at Alexandria in Egypt by a German submarine. There are reported to be over four hundred officers and men killed and about one hundred injured and rescued."

"Let's hope that Dad is safe." We didn't sleep much that night with worry about Dad. We got a telegram the next day informing us that Dad had been rescued but had a slight injury and was being treated on a hospital ship. We learned later that Dad had injured his knee while clambering into a lifeboat. Because of his injury, he could no longer continue in his present role as stoker and was posted to HMS Titania on the River Clyde in Scotland as an Engineer's Writer. The Titania was a submarine depot ship that serviced and repaired damaged submarines. Dad wrote to us and said that it was rumoured that Hitler was planning another big raid on London with some super weapons. He wrote to say that he had found some suitable accommodation in a place called Sandbank in the Holy Loch near him and would we like to come up and live there while the war lasted. It seemed a good idea, and Mum and I soon found ourselves on a train to Scotland. Sandbank was a small village on the banks of the Holy Loch, an offshoot of the Firth of Clyde. It was a very pretty village, but it was rather small. (See map.) It had a population of just over 1,000 inhabitants and had little in the way of shops or places of entertainment. However, this was my first trip to Scotland, and I was overwhelmed by the sight of the mountains, lakes, and pine-covered hills. I had never seen anything quite like it in Brixton! It was beautiful. I had the opportunity to go down to the loch-side and float my model boat, something I had never been able to do back home. I could go to bed at night and have no fear of being bombed; however, the German bombers often did bomb the shipyards in the city of Glasgow. Here we had no anti-aircraft gunfire, no air-raid warnings, no air-raid shelters, no gas masks, and no shrapnel to find in the streets in the morning. You could also buy ice cream here, which you could not do in London. There was one natural occurrence that amazed me. It was something that I had never seen in London: the beautiful multi-coloured Aurora Borealis. I especially liked it when Mum and Dad took us for walks through the Fairy Glen woods on the hillside overlooking the Loch. One eventful day, Mum received a letter from Gran informing her that the bombing in London now was getting rare, with air raids sometimes weeks apart. Mum thought that Gran's letter was very enticing and persuaded Dad that she would like us to return to London, as it seemed quite safe now. She moaned, "It rains every day here, and there is nothing exciting to do."

Dad was not very pleased about this, as he was sure that Hitler had 'something up his sleeve'. Mum eventually won the argument, and we soon caught the train back to London. When we arrived back in Brixton, I noticed that a lot had changed. Some houses that I used to know had been bombed, and only the wreckage remained. My school had been untouched. We soon settled in; I enjoyed going shopping in the big stores in town and enjoyed finding my old toys intact in my toy cupboard. I never realised that I had missed them. Daylight bombings were rare nowadays, but one morning after an 'Alert' wailed its warning, a flight of German warplanes flew over us, but it did not drop any bombs on us. Unfortunately, Hitler did have 'something up his sleeve', as Dad had prophesied. My secondary school history teacher taught me that Hitler was dissatisfied with the attacks by the Luftwaffe on London, Coventry, Liverpool, Hull, and elsewhere. In an air raid, the Luftwaffe would now lose two aircraft for every one RAF fighter. It was becoming too expensive to attack Britain in the old way. Hitler demanded that his scientists come up with some new ideas. They answered his demand and invented the V1, commonly called the flying bomb, buzz bomb, or, more often, the Doodlebug. It was a small pilotless aircraft powered by a jet engine on top. It carried a 2,000 lb high explosive bomb. In the beginning, most of them were to be launched from a base in Peenemünde in Germany. But later, many sites were erected in various parts of Europe. The V1 was mostly aimed at London. The weapon was positioned on a ramp, and the jet engine on top was ignited, sending the V1 on its flight to the proposed target. When the engine ran out of fuel, it would drop on random targets. The first one to arrive was in July 1944 and dropped in the countryside at Swanscombe in Kent. My first sight of the Doodlebug happened one evening. Mum and I had responded to the dreaded air raid siren and were hurriedly making our way to Gran and Grandad's to join them in their shelter. As we walked, we realised that we could hear a throbbing sound in the distance. The sound got nearer, and when we looked up, we saw what looked like a small aeroplane with a jet of flames coming from 'something' on its top. We presumed it was a damaged aircraft crawling its way home to safety. The next morning, in the daily papers, it was announced that the 'plane' was the first flying bomb or V1 to reach London. Although the V1 was pilotless and could not aim at a particular target, it caused a great deal of damage to property and life. It is recorded that 6,725 V1s dropped on England, with 2,340 on London, resulting in 5,476 deaths and 16,000 injured. The most frightening event connected to a V1 that sticks in my memory happened that summer. I was walking home from school when an air raid siren sounded. I was not too concerned, as daylight air raids were quite rare now, and I could not see any sign of enemy aircraft in the sky. Nevertheless, I quickened my pace and headed for home as fast as I could. Suddenly, right in front of me at the end of the street, I saw a dreaded V1 flying bomb appear over the roofs of the houses. I thought that if the engine stopped now, I would be in the direct path of the falling bomb. The engine did stop! I knew from the newspapers that it would take up to 14 seconds before the craft hit the ground, and I now had to decide what to do to avoid death or serious injury from the blast of the 2,000 lb high explosive bomb. It was common wisdom that you should run towards the bomb in the hope that it would glide over you. I had to make a decision in a split second, but I was paralysed to the spot with fear. There was no brick public shelter nearby for me to hide in. The V1 stalled and started to fall towards me, but then, as my hope was fading, the craft banked to the right and glided away over the house tops, and I heard it explode in the distance several seconds later. (It may have been the same one that killed 26 people in Stockwell, south Brixton, that day.) I was never more grateful to get safely home. Dad was very concerned about my safety and suggested that we leave bomb-ridden London and come live in Scotland again. After giving it some thought, we decided it might be a good idea, but Mum insisted that she would not go back to lonely Sandbank. Dad found us some furnished accommodation in the village of Kirn, a few miles south of Sandbank. The village was much larger than our first home and had several shops and amenities that were lacking at the submarine base. I liked it more than Sandbank, as the view overlooked the Firth of Clyde, where the large warships were anchored. I had only seen photographs of them in the newspapers or on Pathe news at the cinema, and now I could see them in real life. I quickly learned the difference between battleships, aircraft carriers, cruisers, destroyers, mine sweepers, and, of course, submarines. My schoolmates in London would have given the earth for the experience of viewing these great ships. There was also a flight of American Catalina seaplanes ("pig boats"), which sought out any German submarines that might attack the ships. Dad would often come home on a 48-hour pass and might take us for a walk along the sea front or even clamber with me over the rocks, looking in the pools for anything interesting. On the 6th of June 1944, D-Day arrived. It was to be the largest seaborne operation ever attempted. Over 132,000 troops from the UK,

USA, Canada, and elsewhere landed on the beaches in several places in Normandy. Hitler was expecting the attacks to be on Calais and was not prepared for the Normandy invasion but still put up a strong resistance. Germany was losing the war, and soon the Allies were capturing V1 launch sites, and attacks on London seemed to be getting less. Apparently, the war was being fought on at least two fronts. The Allies were winning in Europe, and Russia was moving fast against its hated enemy. I understood little about the war, and I wondered when it might finish. We received a letter from Gran telling us that the V1 raids were getting less and less and that it might soon be safe for us to return home. Mum and Dad decided that we should leave peaceful Scotland and go back to Brixton when Dad had some leave due. I was reluctant to leave my earthly paradise, but as the war looked like finishing soon, I could understand that the time was right to return home. Before and after the D-Day landings, there were many American servicemen at bases in Britain, so the sight of an American serviceman was not uncommon. They were well-received by all, and many young women met and married a serviceman and moved to America after the war. My school friends and I would often sit on a wall at the top of Brixton Hill and cheer at the passing lorries carrying the American soldiers to various destinations in Europe. We would scream, "Got any gum, chum!" It was difficult for them to understand our complicated currency, so different from the simple American decimalised one. In Britain, we had ten different metal coins and three paper notes, plus one coin, the guinea, that went out of circulation in 1814 but was still in use today in cattle and racehorse markets. Servicemen had to remember that there were 240 pennies and twenty shillings to the pound and that there were two types of threepenny piece—one silver and one nickel brass—and that there were 80 such coins to the pound! This was all simplified when Britain decimalised its currency in 1979. Back in Germany, the V1 flying bomb was proving to be very expensive to make and not very accurate, and many of the V1 bases were being captured by the UK and her allies. Hitler began looking for something that might do some real damage and perhaps change the course of the war. Unfortunately, his scientists did find something. The second of Hitler's Vengeance weapons was the V2. Hitler called upon the eminent scientist Werner Von Braun to produce a missile that could hit London. It was reckoned that Braun was responsible for Germany being at least 10 years in front of the Americans in the space race. After many expensive experiments, he produced the V2, the world's first ballistic long-range guided missile. It was as high as a four-story building and full of high explosive material. It could travel three times the speed of sound, and the RAF and allied fighters failed to shoot any down. When it was launched, it went straight up into space, turned around, and fell vertically on its target. It was not dirigible, but as long as it fell somewhere in London, the Germans were pleased. It was more frightening than the V1 because you could always hear a V1 coming by the throbbing of its jet engine, but a V2 came silently, and when it crashed, it did considerable damage. The first one to hit London was on July 8th, 1944. It crashed in Chiswick and killed three people. After the war, Werner Von Braun was 'exported' to the USA together with other rocket scientists. He later played a major part in the space race. Mum and Dad decided to leave war-torn London once again. This time we took Gran with us to keep Mum from being lonely.

Dad found us a very nice house in the seaside town of Dunoon, lower down the Firth from Kirn. It was a large town with over 25,000 inhabitants. It contained many large shops, a cinema, a swimming pool, and all the amenities that Mum was used to back home in London. In later years, it became the centre of the tourist trade for that part of Scotland. I made friends with an English boy, Roger Oxland, who lived a few doors away from us. We played together a lot. He had a pre-war copy of Monopoly, which we enjoyed. Dad tried to buy me one, but he was unsuccessful due to the paper shortage. We decided that we would like to go to school. I had not attended one for three months in case Mum did not like Dunoon and wanted to return to London. We obtained two places at Dunoon Grammar School, where we soon settled in. The quality of education in Scotland was higher than in London, and I had to work hard to bring myself up to the standard required. My teacher insisted that I 'rolled my r's' and learned to speak proper Scottish! When I restarted school again in London, I found that I was now about a year ahead of my fellow students. This helped me later to pass the 11-plus examination and gain a place at the Strand Grammar School in Brixton.

On this, our last expected visit to Scotland, our next-door neighbours came out to see us off. To my surprise, Beryl, my next-door playmate, came over and gave me a big kiss on my cheek. I was so embarrassed that I did not know what to say. We agreed, however, to write to each other, but we never did. I took my bicycle with me this time, and my friends and I used to go cycling in the surrounding countryside in search of rose hips, which we collected for a local charity. Apart from rose hips, I once gathered a large bunch of bluebells. When I took them home, Gran nearly had a fit. "You can't bring them in here!" she exclaimed.

"It's very unlucky to bring wildflowers into your house." How was I to know? I was just a young townie from London! We believed that the war was soon coming to an end, but Hitler had another weapon up his sleeve. It was the V3. This was to be a huge cannon. It was to be located underground at the old Mymoyecues Fortress near Calais. Hitler planned to shoot giant high-explosive shells continuously at London until it was completely devastated. After destroying London, the cannon would be aimed at other cities. It would change the conduct of the war. Fortunately, it never had the chance to be used. Once British Intelligence were aware of it, it sent the famous Dam-buster squadron to drop 80 giant 22,000-pound 'Tallboy' earth-penetration bombs on the factory. It succeeded in its mission, but over 300 slave workers were killed as the factory collapsed. We knew nothing about this until after the war had ended. There was talk later that the German scientists had been developing an atomic bomb like the ones to be dropped on Japan, but the story may not have been true. In May 1945, it was VE Day in Europe. Hitler had been conquered and had committed suicide. It was rumoured that he had, in fact, secretly fled to South America, but this was never proven. There were VE street parties everywhere, mainly for children. We even had a bonfire in the street, and it melted the tar surface! War continued in the Far East until the USA dropped two atomic bombs on Japan in June, and they surrendered. Mum and Dad agreed that it was now safe to go home to London. I was sorry in one way as I liked the life in Scotland, and I was sad to say goodbye to my new friends. However, I looked forward to meeting up with Beryl again. It seems that the old saying might have some truth in it:

‘absence makes the heart grow fonder’. I bought her a little woollen Scottish terrier doll as a present. We took the train to London and then to Brixton. We arrived in the evening, and after a fish and chip supper, we went to our welcome beds. The next morning, after a late breakfast, I looked out of the kitchen window and saw a gentleman clipping hedges in Beryl’s garden. I could wait no longer to see her, and I hurriedly made my way into the garden. “Hello,” I called to the stranger. “I am Ron from next door. May I ask who you are?”

“Hello,” he replied, “I’m John, your new neighbour. We moved in recently after the house became vacant.”

“Oh,” I said. “Do you know where they have moved to?”

“Er, I don’t suppose you have heard the news?” he said.

“Mrs Clark and young Beryl went to visit an aunt in Dulwich a little while ago, and no sooner had they got there when a dreaded V2 rocket came out of the clouds and struck the house, and sadly killed them all.” I was shocked and overcome with grief. I wanted to cry, so I went into our outside toilet and sat down and let my tears flow. My grief at losing Beryl was even greater than that I had ever experienced, even more than the death of my pilot friend John. Of course, Beryl’s woollen Scotty dog never found a new home. I learned that there are no victors in war. Both the British and the Allies and the Germans lost husbands, wives, sons, daughters, and friends. I hoped that when I grew up, I would never have to serve in any military force. (When I reached eighteen years of age, I was called up to serve two years of National Service with the RAF.) Life was not the same after the war. It got better for our family. Dad was home from the Royal Navy and soon got employment as a boiler-man, earning good wages.

The Council promised us a new flat or a 'prefab,' and Mum got pregnant with my new brother, John. A few days after we had returned to London, Mum and Dad said to me one evening, "Let's go downtown and see the lights." We went, and I wondered what I was to see. Much to my amazement, all the shops in Brixton High Street and surrounding areas had their large front windows lit up so that we could see all their wares. I remembered that when the war began, we turned off our lights. Now that the war was over, we switched them on again. Truly, I was no longer 'A Child at War'.

The End

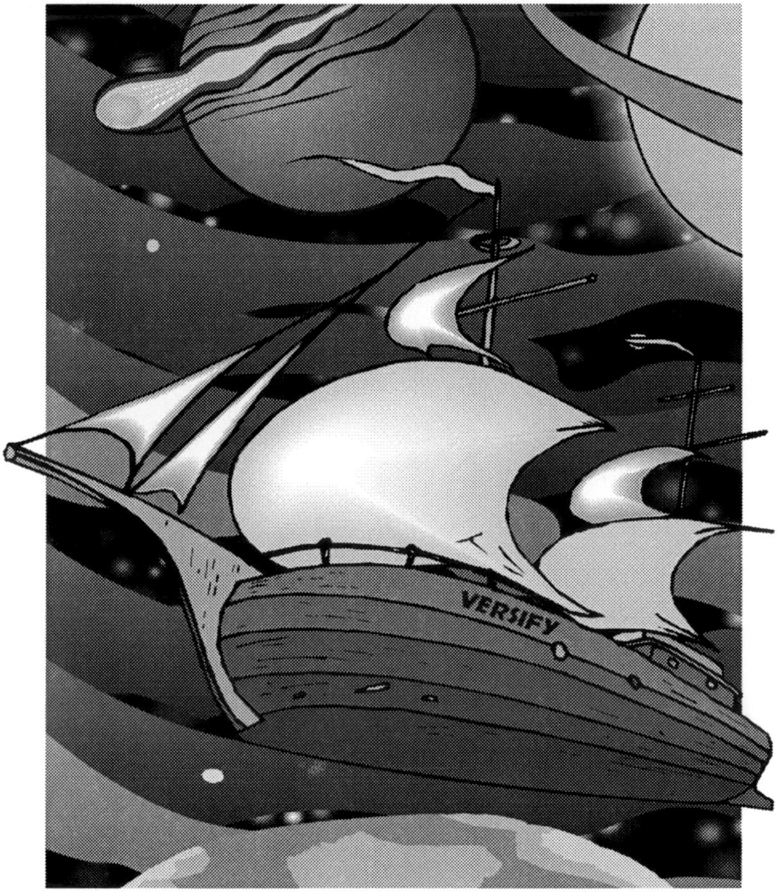

POETIC VOYAGES SUTTON COLDFIELD

Edited by Heather Killingray

First published in Great Britain in 2001 by
YOUNG WRITERS
Remus House,
Coltsfoot Drive,
Peterborough, PE2 9JX
Telephone (01733) 890066

HB ISBN 0 75432 598 9
SB ISBN 0 75432 599 7

FOREWORD

Young Writers was established in 1991 with the aim to promote creative writing in children, to make reading and writing poetry fun.

This year once again, proved to be a tremendous success with over 88,000 entries received nationwide.

The Poetic Voyages competition has shown us the high standard of work and effort that children are capable of today. It is a reflection of the teaching skills in schools, the enthusiasm and creativity they have injected into their pupils shines clearly within this anthology.

The task of selecting poems was therefore a difficult one but nevertheless, an enjoyable experience. We hope you are as pleased with the final selection in *Poetic Voyages Sutton Coldfield* as we are.

Contents

The Poems

THE OCEAN, THE EARTH

It is cold, frightening, but fearful,
The fishes are lovely and cheerful,
But the sharks are horrible and fearful,
And the seaweed sways all day long.

It is cold, frightening, but fearful,
The fishes are nasty and dull,
But the sharks are friendly and cheerful,
And the seaweed stays where it is.

It is sunny, playful and breezy,
Where children play all day long,
It is sunny, playful and windy,
Where adults rest all day long.

Louise Mitcham (9)
Banners Gate Junior School

YELLOW SUBMARINE

One day I went floating in the sea,
When all of a sudden something grabbed hold of me,
I went down, down the sea
Until down as can be.
I saw fishes and a yellow submarine.
It took me aboard, I went to the torpedo room
And saw the torpedoes ready to fire
And the captain was dressed in a white uniform
With a black tic.
I will never forget the things I saw
Aboard the yellow submarine.

David Wood (9)
Banners Gate Junior School

SPACE

I went up, up and away
Cool! I saw the stars, wow!
I must be in space

Mars as red as fire.

Venus as orange as a tomato.

Earth as blue as blueberries.

Mercury as white as nothing.

Jupiter as red as a strawberry.

Saturn as yellow as sand.

Neptune as blue as a blue chair.

Samantha Blount (10)
Banners Gate Junior School

THE BESTEST DREAM

One night I had the bestest dream
taking off to the moon.
Getting ready, starting up,
zooming off, counting down.
People looking up and down.
Everybody shouting 'Yahoo, off we go.'
Higher and higher, on the way to try to name them
we say Mercury, Venus, Mars, Earth,
Jupiter, Saturn, Uranus, Neptune, Pluto.

Faye Mansell (10)
Banners Gate Junior School

Sailing The Caribbean

As I sailed the Caribbean
I saw
Patterned, rough shells
As big as clams
Super swimming fishermen
Diving off their boats
Multicoloured speedy fish
Sparkling in the water
Transparent sparkly water
Flowing round my boat
Big beautiful cruise liners
Sailing in the ocean
Huge sandy islands
Covered with people
Beautiful palm trees
Swaying in the wind.

Joshua Gahir (8)
Banners Gate Junior School

Sailing In The Caribbean

As I sailed the Caribbean I saw
A great big fish
As shiny as the sun.
Clear blue water
That has the waves in.
Swaying seaweed
Swishing side to side.
Nice shiny sand
As shiny as glitter.
A fish as long as a palm tree
With shiny scales.

Daniel James (8)
Banners Gate Junior School

BACK IN WONDERLAND

Where on a magic carpet
Back to Wonderland
Two mad professors moaning at each other
Like little children
King Arthur fighting his wars
Round and round I go
Into the next century.
World War I has started, *bang*, gun firing.
World War II has finished, nothing is left of London.
Going round, going to the Wonderland section.
Aliens have landed, everybody's going crazy.
Saturn's singing, Mars is mourning,
Mercury's up to mischief,
Earth is expelled,
Jupiter's junk, Pluto's being pushed,
Venus has vanished, Neptune's nibbling
Uranus under an umbrella.
Now I'm going back to Earth.

James Heath (9)
Banners Gate Junior School

IMAGINATION

As I lay there on my bed,
I close my eyes and dream.
I use my imagination,
What mystical things will I see?

Wizards and witches and dragons galore,
Breathtaking creatures (there's lots).
Remarkable things you could only dream of,
They're stunning, the big and the small.

Drifting through an immense universe,
Watching the stars flashing by.
Aimlessly coasting beyond the unknown,
Oh, this is the life that I like!

Dreaming of the future,
Imagining the past.
Futuristic cities,
Oh, I wish that this could last!

Thomas Smith (10)
Banners Gate Junior School

Madene

There was a lady called Madene
Who travelled in a time machine
She landed on the planet Zon
It was a very yellow planet
It even had volcanoes on
She smelt a very cheesy breeze
For the planet was made of cheese
She met some monsters on the planet
One called Mr Slime, another Canet
She met a holly bird called Flippy Flop
It showed her to the castle Zop
It was scary and exciting
And it was frightening
She lived there for evermore
She didn't like the paving stones on the floor
She lived there with the queen Enchanter
And lived happily ever after.

Michael Evans (9)
Banners Gate Junior School

Sailing The Caribbean

As I sailed the Caribbean
I saw

Hard rough shells
Lying on the beach,
Tall green trees
A dark green colour,
Beautiful tall people
Lying on the beach,
Clear blue water
Reflecting me.

Beautiful colourful fish
Swimming in the sea,
High white birds
Flying above the sea,
Green-grey island
Beautiful as could be,
Brown sharp crabs
Shipping at me.

Andrew Donaldson (9)
Banners Gate Junior School

As I Sailed Around St Lucia I Saw . . .

Happy, smiling faces
White sandy beaches
Large blue sharks
Big rocky mountains
Great tall palm trees
Deep blue sea.

Andrew Anderson (9)
Banners Gate Junior School

Sailing The Caribbean Sea

As I sailed the Caribbean I saw
Soft, silky seaweed
Shiny, colourful shells
Old, brown boats
Large, green palm trees

Orange rough crabs
Multicoloured, sparkling fish
Dashing through the sea
Beautiful, famous butterflies
Floating in the air
Kind, respectful people
Playing catch
Hard bumpy stones just lying there
Little brown villages

Tiny little islands while sand falling off
Dark, large coral
Not doing anything
Flowing, swaying seaweed
Moving side to side
Spiky, hairy seaweed looking like thorns.

Lauren Keight (8)
Banners Gate Junior School

Poetic Voyages

As I sailed around St Lucia
I saw happy, smiling faces,
white sandy beaches
deep blue sea
long rocky beaches
brown-green palm trees.

Brandon Valentine (9)
Banners Gate Junior School

Magical Land

Deep beneath the sea,
Further than you can see,
There's a magical land,
Deeper than the sand.
A land that is round,
Dogs will not pound.
You will see!
People who are happy,
You don't change a nappy.
Do anything you want,
Even change the font.
Buy anything you need,
No one will greed.

Owain Jones (10)
Banners Gate Junior School

Sailing The Caribbean Sea

As I sailed the Caribbean I saw
Strong dirty shells
Very clear water
Flowing beautifully
Beautiful, loving people
Beautiful, colourful birds
Beautiful, swooping birds
Loving land
Big brown and green trees.

Tasha Wall (8)
Banners Gate Junior School

As I Sailed Around St Lucia I Saw . . .

Big rocky mountains
Jumping blue dolphins
Buzzy busy bees
Happy laughing faces
Large blue sharks
Funny shaped shells
White sandy beaches
Smooth blue dolphins
Fat, ugly fishes
Colourful flying butterflies
Silly fat pigeons
Big juicy fruits
Cute baby dolphins
Big brown rocks
Three lovely birds
Little round apples.

Hayley Patterson (9)
Banners Gate Junior School

As I Sailed Around St Lucia

As I sailed around St Lucia I saw
a big cruise ship
big floppy dolphins
big red fish
large blue sharks
Big rocky mountains
Great tall palm trees
white sandy beaches
deep blue sea.

Jason Langsford (8)
Banners Gate Junior School

Sailing Around St Lucia I Saw . . .

Deep turquoise sea
white sandy beaches
spiky black sea urchins
large grey sharks
smooth fragile shells
bright blue dolphins
sparkly shiny fish
big cruise ships
great tall palm trees
smooth yellow bananas
hairy rough coconuts
ripe juicy apples
black Caribbean people
bright wooden houses
hot rocky volcanoes
and big rocky Pitons.

Katie Wright (9)
Banners Gate Junior School

Poetic Voyages

I went to see an alien under water,
He shouted 'Goodbye,' and gave me a pie.
He said 'Come in and shut the door,
Do you want some more tea?'
I said 'No,' and he brought me some more!

He took me fishing. When he got a bite he let the rod go.
When we went hunting he shot the tree instead of the bird!
He said, 'We are going diving,' but he took me up to space,
We both said, 'We are going,' but he went to the Dome!

We went to the pictures tomorrow,
And got a front seat at the back!
He drank the popcorn and ate the pop bottle with the pop in
I watched him fall asleep with his eyes open.

Simon Ashcroft (10)
Banners Gate Junior School

SAILING THE CARIBBEAN

As I sailed the Caribbean
I saw
Shimmering, clear water
Bluer than the sky
Scaly, sparkling fish
Darting through the waves
Rough, multicoloured shells
Deep beneath the water
Beautiful, gliding birds
Sailing in the air
Floating olive seaweed
Climbing up the boat
Fantastic golden sand
Sitting near the shore
Wooden fishing boats
Floating away nearby
Energetic, sneaky animals
Prowling in the sun
Magnificent tall palm trees
Blowing in the breeze
Terrific, noisy cruise liners
Gliding in the water.

Olivia Ward (8)
Banners Gate Junior School

UNDERNEATH THE SEA

I'm underneath the sea,
Nobody else but me
But then a dragon came whizzing past me.
I felt scared, I think you would be.
I swam down to the ocean floor
And into a cave it was dark
But at the back of the cave
There were some sweets and treasure.
I kept some sweets and some gold
And carried on back through the cave
But then something big and smelly appeared,
A scaly sea dragon, its scales were mouldy and slimy.
It was walking towards me, probably trying to eat me
But then a big gust of wind blew me to the shore
And I never saw the sea dragon again.
What a relief.

Emma Smith (10)
Banners Gate Junior School

JUST STAY IN BED

One day I went to Mars to have a look at the stars,
but all I could see
was a big, round tree
that was six foot three.

One day I went to Saturn
to have a look at the pattern,
but all I could see
was a big bumblebee,
and then I said 'I'll go to bed,
and stay there from all this mess.'

Thomas Tubb (10)
Banners Gate Junior School

UNDER THE SAND

In the ocean,
Under the sand,
There is a land,
Where nobody knows,
Where everyone is loving and kind,
You never die,
And you can fly,
But one interesting boom,
Happens every time fear enters,
Fear is eight foot long, spotty, disgusting, terrifying, strings,
They look like legs or some sort of fish
But that only happens once a year,
And then the most perfect thing of all,
Is how they talk,
It's funny and rhymes,
There are no crimes,
And that is the best world of all!

Matthew Hipkiss (10)
Banners Gate Junior School

THE STRANGE FAMILY

We went to the moon and heard a tune
And the stars were sparkling on Mars.
Then we were near the sun
Then we saw my mum.
After, we went to the sun
My mother hit my brother
Then we split up and my mother went to Earth
But she was glad to go.
Then me and my brother went to see the man on the moon,
But the man on the moon was . . . an alien we didn't know.

Laura Swain (9)
Banners Gate Junior School

UNTITLED

Gliding as fast as I can
past enormous fishes and whales and things
you can't see
you will never see what I will see.

Through dark water and light water
go, go fast as I can.
Swirling through
on my own in thin air.

I'm half way there now
I can't wait
gliding and smiling
and wow, never seen that fish before.

Dodging here and there
getting hit and bit
fishes stopping to
stare and some
even had hair.

I'm tired now, I'll be there soon
I'm so tired, I can't wait to have a rest.

I'll be the best.

There it is, I'm there, yes
I'm the best you see.

Harry Cobley (9)
Banners Gate Junior School

SAILING IN THE CARIBBEAN

As I sailed the Caribbean
I saw
Soft silky seaweed
Flowing in the sea.
Flowing black seaweed
As dark as could be.
Hard, cold shells
On the shore.
Long bright palm trees
On the side.
Gigantic, strong animals
Drinking out of the sea.
Kind, respectful people
In the sea.
Beautiful bright fishes
Please come to me.
Cute, tall birds
Sitting on the shore.
Tiny little islands
Far, far away.
Large pieces of coral
In the sea.
Spiky hairy seaweed
Like my brother's hair.
Dark green seaweed
Like the colour of my costume.

Jodie Deathridge (9)
Banners Gate Junior School

As I Sailed Around St Lucia I Saw . . .

Nice colourful people,
happy, smiling faces
white sandy beaches
large blue sharks
big colourful school
big rocky mountains
great tall trees
deep blue sea
small yellow fish
big long swordfish
big green trees
little red volcano
juicy yummy coconuts
big bright sun
big nice fruits.

Knikita Lindo (8)
Banners Gate Junior School

Sailing The Caribbean

As I sailed the Caribbean sea
I saw a big coral and
A big dog fish.
I saw a jelly fish.
I saw a very big crab.
I saw a boy swimming in the water
And I saw a big, big bird.
I saw big huts on the island.
In the water I saw a big, big ship.
A catfish in the water.
I saw a big rock and
I saw the Caribbean.

James Bibb (9)
Banners Gate Junior School

The Trip To Cadbury World

I'm on the planet Saturn,
on my way beyond space,
wondering where I'll go,
flying past the other planets,
and just viewing stars all around me.
Being dragged to the side by a black hole,
now wedged in something brown
that has wedged the door.
I destroyed the window and I jumped out.
Holding books of planets and trees and places,
opening up the book of 'Places in Black Holes'
and in front of me grew the woggle plant.
All around me I saw a wiggle waggle, woggle plant.
The plain plant,
the nut plant,
the flow plant
and the golden net plant.
Everything I saw was made of chocolate.

Stephen Harrison (9)
Banners Gate Junior School

The Jumping Aliens

Zooming through space I smelt the burning sun
It was very hot.
I heard some jumping aliens getting closer and closer.
I tasted burning things,
I didn't know what they were
So I smelt it again.
I thought it smelt like aliens.
The satellite was buzzing and humming.

Rachael Taylor (8)
Banners Gate Junior School

The Trip

It's a cold winter morning,
Mum's packing my things.
I'm very afraid of what the future may bring.
I'm going to the station
When the siren rings.
I'm very afraid of what the future may bring.

We leave the cellar
And rush to the station.
A big black train is waiting to leave,
Mum kisses me
And waves goodbye.
The big black train is leaving.

I find a compartment
All to myself,
But shortly I am joined by someone else.
We make friends and play games
And have lots of fun.
But shortly we are joined by someone else.

This kid we see
Is five foot three
And beats the living daylights out of me.
He hits me here,
He hits me there
And beats the living daylights out of me.

We arrive at six minutes past three,
It's now colder than before.
We wait on platform 4 to be collected.
This lady comes
And chooses me.
We walk off platform 4.

Freya Daniel (10)
Banners Gate Junior School

ONE DAY

It's a scary life
Being in the war
All running when we hear the sirens
Mothers crying, children wearing gas masks
Bombs being dropped all the time
Here comes the train, the long train.

I am on the train
Waving goodbye to my family
My family are blurring
With a tear in my eye
Waving goodbye makes them and me cry
Saying goodbye will never end.

The train is making a lot of noise
Just sitting here listening
It sounds as if it's stopping
The man is blowing a whistle
Every minute of the way
The sounds are loud around me.

This train is very dusty
It smells horrid
The other children smell too
We are all hot and quiet.
Everyone smells of gas
From the gas bombs.

The train is slowing down
It's getting slower, slower . . . stopped
Everyone is quiet getting off the train
Once we were all off the train
We marched round and round
Finally I was picked to go to the nice lady's house.

Amy Rowan (10)
Banners Gate Junior School

Willie The Evacuee

The day has come,
I'm walking to the train station,
Everyone's sobbing,
Or crying,
I'm parting from Mom,
For the very first time,
It's crowded all round,
It's time to go.

All us children are holding on the train,
Gathering round windows,
To wave goodbye,
Hang on a minute,
Where's Mom,
She's gone,
I wave anyway,
The train has started.

You can hear the train whistle go,
Choo! Choo! Choo choo!
There's a rumbling sound,
Some children are crying,
Some excited,
What should I do?
It's weird,
What should I feel?

I've got off the train,
A lady runs to us,
We follow her,
I'm at the back of the line,
We go round houses,
It's my turn now, she knocks,
A man enters, I go in,
Should I be glad or sad?

My journey's over,
I go to bed, I say to the man,
'Goodnight Mr Tom,'
He replied, 'Goodnight Willie.'

Sophie Gardner
Banners Gate Junior School

EVERYTHING IN SPACE

Zooming through space I . . .
See silver spaceships blasting
Round space station twirling
Spotty aliens partying.

Zooming through space I . . .
Touch the glistening moon of silver
Dark black comets shooting
Spiky stars playing.

Zooming through space I . . .
Hear green aliens chattering
Red sun frazzling
Sparkly shooting stars floating.

Zooming through space I . . .
Smell smoky sun
Small engines
Burning meteorites

Zooming through space I . . .
Taste sugary moondust exploding
Aliens' eyeballs of goo
Food from space station.

Jodie Ford (7)
Banners Gate Junior School

THE JOURNEY

There was a man called Stan
who wanted to travel to the Isle of Man.

He set off with his waterproof coat
travelling on his big brown boat.

There was a massive storm;
it finished when it was dawn.

He found he was on an unknown island
he looked on his map, it wasn't Germany, France or Thailand.

He heard a roaring sound;
he couldn't see anything on the ground.

He looked up above
and he thought to himself it was a giant dove.

He was shaking,
you would have thought the ground was quaking.

He got sticks and stones
to break its bones.

The thing flew off in the sky
now he was thinking of a signal to get help from passers by.

Now he thought of a solution, make a fire!
He was so happy he started singing songs that he sang in the choir.

When he was sleeping a helicopter flew by
the massive fire caught the pilot's eye.

The helicopter picked up Stan
and the pilot said, 'I don't think you'll be going to the Isle of Man.'

Robert Holder (10)
Banners Gate Junior School

LEAVING HOME

Drip drop went the rain on this gloomy day
Apparently we were being
Boarded off to a place a long way away
My mom was sad and so was I
I was leaving her for the first time
I was told not to be sad but to be bright
I thought I was going to be gone for one night
As the days went past
I got very sad and could not concentrate
This meant I did bad and never passed my grade

This meant that I was left back a grade
I tried so hard I became a slave
The man who looked after me
Made me work all day
Then on one cold and windy day I passed 4th grade
So I wrote to my mom to tell her this
But no one wrote back
I was sad about this
The man I was staying with said I would never see my mom again
But I was sure I'd see her again

As the days went past I got very tired
I could not work
For I was so tired
But it did not stop me trying to work
Until one day the train came and I went home
I was no longer a slave
But I was looking forward to what I would see
But when I got home my mom was waiting for me
Just as I had thought she would be.

Matthew Donaldson (11)
Banners Gate Junior School

Leavin' Town

We've practised marchin' up and down
But today we're goin' to be leavin' town.
Standin' still in a crocodile line,
Till the teacher says it's time.
Feelin' scared and very frightened,
All of a sudden me tummy's tightened.

Gas mask 'angin' from me arm,
We might need them at the farm.
Wrote me own name on a label,
(Did it at the kitchen table).
It's got a little splodge of jam,
('ome-made, got it from me gran).

Marched as quietly down the street,
Sat on the bus next to me mate Pete.
Excited goin' on the train,
Even when it began to rain.
We 'ave stopped, don't know where,
Tired and starvin' 'ope we're there.

'Uddled in an old church 'all,
Size of it makes me feel small.
The sign says 'Pick your own evacuee',
'Ope the jolly lady chooses me.
Me an' Pete can't believe our luck,
As we jump in the back of 'er truck.

Didn't know there was this much green,
An' other colours I've never seen.
Mrs Shaw works us really 'ard,
Diggin', sweepin' and cleanin' the yard.
But if we do all she says,
She'll take us blackberry pickin' one of these days.

It's bin a year since I've seen Mom,
Last night our 'ouse was 'it by a bomb!
Anderson shelter saved me mom,
And Mrs Shaw said she can come.
Mum can 'elp 'er run the farm,
She says a bit more 'elp wouldn't do 'ny 'arm.

Thinkin' 'bout Dad, 'ope 'e's okay,
P'raps 'e'll come to the country one day.

Antony Barker (11)
Banners Gate Junior School

SAILING AROUND ST LUCIA

As I sailed around St Lucia I saw . . .
Large bushy palm trees
Gold sandy beaches
Ripe tempting fruit
Bright blazing sun
Deep salty sea
Steaming fiery volcanoes
Giant rocky mountains
Big juicy coconuts
Cheery red crabs
Long yellow bananas
Pretty pink shells
Nice tasty mangoes
Funny smiley people
Gliding smooth dolphins
Silky white sands
And grey ugly *sharks!*

Sally Hurrell Woodward (8)
Banners Gate Junior School

GOING THROUGH SPACE

Zooming through space . . .
I see dark aliens walking in space
Bright stars gleaming and the moon

Zooming through space . . .
I touch large comets flying
A green alien walking

Zooming through space . . .
I hear aliens chatting to each other
Plants moving around

Zooming through space . . .
I smell burning sun smoke
Alien slime

Zooming through space . . .
I taste sugary moondust
Alien slime.

Stacey Hansen (7)
Banners Gate Junior School

SPACE

Zooming through space
I see little furry aliens waiting for me.
See the smoky sun.
Touch the big spaceship.
Hear green aliens screaming.
Hear squeaking spaceships.
Smell of aftershave.
Taste sugary moondust.

Sam Wegrzynowski (7)
Banners Gate Junior School

In Space

Zooming through space I see
Huge planets whizzing past me
And I see the high moon winking at me
In the dark, black sky high above me.

Zooming through space I touch
The sparkling shooting stars
That fly past me in my huge rocket ship
And I touch the red-hot sun that was flying past me.

Zooming through space I hear
Ugly, slimy green aliens fighting on the moon
And I hear the shooting stars
Floating past me.

Zooming through space I smell
The smoky red-hot sun
Floating through the air.

Zooming through space I taste
The saucy moondust flying through
The window of my spaceship.

Hayley Wood (8)
Banners Gate Junior School

Space Poem

Zooming through space, I smell the burning sun.
I see bright stars gleaming bright up in the sky.
I hear ugly aliens chattering loud, up so high in the sky.
I smell the stinky, smoky, shining sun,
I taste the sugary moondust, it tastes horrible.

Rhys Roberts (7)
Banners Gate Junior School

Sailing Around St Lucia

As I sailed around
St Lucia I saw . . .
Big rocky mountains
Large blue sharks
Big juicy fruits
White sandy beaches
Great tall palm trees
Deep blue sea
Smooth grey dolphins
Happy joyful faces
Shiny smooth shells
Wide blue sky
Rough round coconuts
Ripe yellow bananas
Big coloured fish.

Rhyanne Cowley (9)
Banners Gate Junior School

Space

Zooming through space
I see the bright, shining moon
And big shiny craters with a big hole
Zooming through space
I touch a very big yellow thing.
It is scorching hot.
Zooming through space
I hear the sound of aliens
Muttering and shouting at each other
Zooming through space I smell the rotten eggs.

Jack Rowan (8)
Banners Gate Junior School

POETIC VOYAGES

As I sailed around
St Lucia I saw
Large blue sharks
Great large palm trees
Deep salty sea
Big rocky mountains
Large juicy mangoes
Big milky coconuts
Big erupting volcanoes
White sandy beaches
Big long bananas
Boiling blazing sun
Glittering blue sharks.

Katharine Corbett (9)
Banners Gate Junior School

ZOOMING THROUGH SPACE

Zooming through space
I see rocky comets flying
Green aliens groaning.
Zooming through space
I touch wiry satellites buzzing
Bright stars floating.
Zooming through space
I hear shiny spaceships flying
Green aliens muttering.
Zooming through space
I smell the smoky sun.

Bradley Fleming (8)
Banners Gate Junior School

Space

Zooming through space I see . . .

Stars sparkling and glittering,
Huge aliens that look horrible and slimy
And the fiery sun burning.

Zooming through space I touch . . .
Comets zooming around me
They feel bumpy and hard.
I couldn't believe I could touch the moon.

I hear chatting, it is aliens,
They have a funny way of talking.

I smell the smoky sun
And the cheesy moondust.

I taste cheese, I taste alien food
I think it is pretty good.
You should go zooming through space too!

Hannah Jones (7)
Banners Gate Junior School

Zooming Through Space

See:
Zooming through space I see
Bright satellites shining
Stars zooming
Floating astronauts falling

Touch:
Zooming through space I will touch
Nasty aliens yapping
Huge comets flying
Shooting stars glowing

Hear:
Zooming through space I hear
Someone whispering in my ear
Hey, it's you!
An alien, help!

Smell:
Zooming through space I smell
Rotten eggs, smells horrible
Smoky sun too
Boy this place stinks!

Celina-Anne Howell (7)
Banners Gate Junior School

SPACE

Zooming through space I
See bright sun gleaming
Light stars shining and
Ugly aliens frightening us

Zooming through space I
Touch giant comets dropping
See spaceships whizzing along and
Green aliens chatting.

Zooming through space I
Hear slimy aliens screaming 'Ahhh!'
Shiny satellites buzzing
Buzz!

Zooming through space I
Smell of aftershave, mmmmm!

Zooming through space I
Taste sugary moondust.

Jack Walker (7)
Banners Gate Junior School

ZOOMING THROUGH SPACE

Zooming through space
I see pretty shiny stars
Shining, gleaming, shooting.

Zooming through space
I touch massive, huge asteroids
Zooming, flying.

Zooming through space
I hear hungry green Martians
Shouting, moaning and groaning.

Zooming through space
I smell the red-hot burning sun.

Zooming through space
I taste sugary sweet moondust
Melting in my mouth.

Emily Villers (8)
Banners Gate Junior School

ZOOMING THROUGH SPACE

Zooming through space I see
Slimy aliens chatting.
Zooming through space I touch
Huge meteors blasting.
Zooming through space I hear
Shiny satellites buzzing.
Zooming through space I smell
Smoky sun burning.
Zooming through space I taste
Sugary moon dust fuzzing.

Joshua Harnett (7)
Banners Gate Junior School

Space Senses

Zooming through space
I see the spiky moon like a statue and
Planets all different colours too.
The ugly aliens staring at us
Frighten us to death to look.

Zooming through space
I touch a spiky star
Prick my finger and it hurts very much.

Zooming through space
I hear the sun beaming
I also hear satellites buzzing away.

Zooming through space
I smell cheese and taste it too.

Sophie Sharpe (7)
Banners Gate Junior School

In Space

Zooming through space
I see green aliens jumping.

Zooming through space
I touch huge comets flying.

Zooming through space
I hear silver satellites buzzing.

Zooming through space
I smell smoky sun burning.

Zooming through space
I taste sugary moondust crackling.

Emma Robbins (7)
Banners Gate Junior School

As I Sailed Around St Lucia I Saw

As I sailed around St Lucia I saw . . .
deep blue sea
big tropical fruits
shining gold shells
tall fat trees
graceful floating clouds
smooth blue dolphins
big fat sharks
fluffy tropical birds
colourful flying butterflies
steep rocky mountains
coloured tiny blow fish.

Rachel Gee (9)
Banners Gate Junior School

Poetic Voyages

As I sailed around
St Lucia I saw . . .

Big, nice dolphins
Big blue sky
Big, colourful mountains
Big, tasty apples
Big, juicy bananas
Blue, dark sea
Brown, green plum trees
Dark brown hotel
Deep blue sea
White sandy beaches.

Jamal Bramwell (9)
Banners Gate Junior School

POETIC VOYAGES

As I sailed around
St Lucia I saw
Bright hot sun,
Blue deep sea,
Big juicy fruits,
White noisy ships,
Big brown rainforest,
Large brown trees,
Hot steamy volcanoes,
Tiny red ants,
Small coloured people,
Small wooden houses,
Shiny silver fish.

Louise Wakefield (9)
Banners Gate Junior School

AS I SAILED AROUND ST LUCIA

As I sailed
around St Lucia
I saw . . .
happy laughing people
tall colourful flags
deep blue sea
large red boats
big hairy crabs
large blue sharks
golden soft sand
small grey fish
tall erupting volcanoes.

Gemma Davies (8)
Banners Gate Junior School

SAILING IN THE CARIBBEAN

As I sailed the Caribbean I saw
Shiny white shells
Lying in the sand.
Dark blue sea
Floating on the sand
Beautiful coloured fishes
In the dark blue sea
Small red crabs
In the beach
Huge green mountains
As high as three houses
Hot orange sun
Floating in the sky
Sinky yellow sand
That will sink your feet right to the ground.

Kirsty McKernan (9)
Banners Gate Junior School

SAILING THE CARIBBEAN

As I sailed the Caribbean I saw
Hard rocky coral
As big as a mountain
Extremely rare birds
As fine as leather
Shining silver fish
Darting through the waves

Lovely hard shells
Some are patterned too
Small tiny islands
Planted in the waves and the sea.

Sam Sharpe (9)
Banners Gate Junior School

POETIC VOYAGES

As I sailed around
St Lucia I saw . . .
Happy smiling faces
White sandy beaches
Grey, dark dolphins
Big emptying volcanoes
Big brown crabs
Deep blue sea
Great tall palm trees
Juicy ripe apples
Large glowing sun
Big rocky mountains
Large blue sharks
Big tall flats
Large grey rocks
Dark blue sea
Enormous cruise ships.

Thomas Harley (9)
Banners Gate Junior School

POETIC VOYAGE

Hello, I am an alien from space.
My name is Benjamin.
I am going to Earth.
I am really scared.
It's my first time.
The sun is really hot.
I just saw a rocket go by, it was fast.
Goodbye, I am going down to Earth.
I am there now.
There are loads of people.

Emma Woolford (9)
Banners Gate Junior School

THE JOURNEY

Don't know where I'm going
I don't know where to go
Maybe I should run
Or maybe I should go slow.

The bus is coming up the road
It's coming very fast
Should I get on
Or will it go past?

I decided not to take the bus
And walk on down the road
I tripped up the gutter
And fell on a toad.

The toad went splat
And I just sat
And looked up in the air
A brolly was what I needed as rain fell on my hair.

The rain is getting heavier
And I begin to run
I wish I'd caught that bus now
Because this is no fun.

I am running up the hill,
As fast as I can go
You would think this is fast
But really it is slow.

Because as I am running I banged my toe.

I'm feeling very tired
After being out all day
I think I should head home now
And go the other way.

I walk across the road
And look back again
Looking for the bus
I hope it's number ten.

The number ten is coming
As I start running
It stops to pick me up
I hope it's not full up,
I sit down on the seat
To rest my weary feet
Start my journey home
But I am not alone!

Michelle Whitehouse (11)
Banners Gate Junior School

UNDER THE SEA

In the sea,
Colourful fish float around me,
Little crabs crawling around,
You can't hear them make a sound.

As I go further down,
All the fishes follow me around,
Further and further as I go,
Deeper and deeper as we float and go low.

As calm as a tree
And as rough as the sea,
Still the fishes float around me.

Rebecca Wilkins (9)
Banners Gate Junior School

MY JOURNEY

After school before it got dark,
My friend and I
Went to the park.

We played on the slide and swings
And all the other
Different things.

After we had played
We made our way home,
On my friend's house
Was a big porch
Shaped like a Dome.

He rang the doorbell,
His mom let us in,
We were so hungry,
We emptied the biscuit tin.

After we ate,
His mom said to me,
You better go home
Before you are late.

On my way home
I heard a dog bark,
And in the sky
I spotted a skylark.

As I walked I passed a shop
So I went inside
And got some pop.

I reached home
And went inside my house,
Quiet as a mouse.

I told my mom I had been fed,
So I went up to bed,
Goodnight.

Nathan Rushton (10)
Banners Gate Junior School

SPACE MISSION

Zooming through space I
See a big sun shining
I touch a massive comet flying
I hear a big meteor coming to get me!

Zooming through outer space I
Hear ugly aliens shouting to each other
I see a space radar shooting a shuttle with his ray gun
I touch the shuttle that is crashing into me
Trying to dodge the bullets.

Zooming through outer space
I smell cold ice from Mars
I taste chalky moondust
From the moon.

Zooming through outer space
I smell slimy aliens groaning
I taste some yucky alien slime.

Joel Evans (7)
Banners Gate Junior School

VOYAGE

Evacuated from my home
Said goodbye to my parents, friends and home
I feel sad and alone
As I waved from the train
It poured with rain
My parents grew smaller and smaller
As I waved and waved from the smoke-blowing train
Into the countryside the train carried me away
To a new place where I had to stay
It was quieter, quieter than ever
No sirens, no bombs, no guns, nothing
Lots of boys and girls looking sad, like me
Wondering where their new homes would be
Passing through large green fields with lots of trees
Seeing cows and sheep running free
Was all new to me
Wondering would I need my gas mask
I carried with me
I was nervous of where I was going to stay
New people, new places
All in one day
I felt sick in a strange sort of way
But it's not forever
I go home some day.

Adam Martin (10)
Banners Gate Junior School

FAR OUT IN THE OCEAN

Far out in the ocean,
Under the waves,
There is a world with beautiful caves,
Go a bit further and you will see,
A sensational pool of swirling blue sea.

Go even further to be amazed
Or some might say to be dazed
A clock strikes twelve, it's lunchtime
Beautiful streaks of golden sunshine
Go even further to be in Spain
The swimming journey was a pain.

Matthew Lee (9)
Banners Gate Junior School

I'M AN EVACUEE

We walked into the school,
People were gathering in the hall.
My teacher stood up and said 'We are going to the train station.'
My parents shouted 'Yippee, we're gonna get compensation.'

Evacuation!
The teacher told us the information.
Children said goodbye to their parents and slowly walked onto the train.
It started to rain and rain.

The train started to go faster and faster.
Children eating food like pasta.
There were animals I've never seen before, only in picture books.
The train stopped, I got my luggage and coat off the hooks.

Children were getting pushed into another little hall,
A boy was playing with his ball.
Lots of people came in and started taking children away.
A man and lady took me out to play.

They took me to their home
Where they offered me a comb.
They were nice and kind
But the old man was nearly blind.

Laura Harley (11)
Banners Gate Junior School

SNIPER, A VOYAGE INTO THE UNKNOWN

Crawling, creeping in the trees,
A voyage into the unknown,
Slowly moving in the breeze.

Silently stalking enemy men,
A voyage into the unknown,
Up on the trees, in the enemy's den.

He's creeping through the plants and flowers,
A voyage into the unknown,
Keeping away from the sentry towers.

Closer, closer to his prey,
A voyage into the unknown,
Coming closer to the end of the day.

The sun is gone, in comes the night,
A voyage into the unknown,
Slowly creeping into the fight.

Gunshot! Red alert! Wound on the head,
A voyage into the unknown,
Snipers aim, one man dead.

Aiming stealthily, one more dead,
A voyage into the unknown,
His brains blew out from a shot in the head.

Running away from the enemies' might,
A voyage into the unknown,
Running away from the awful fight.

Losing his courage, losing his mind,
A voyage into the unknown,
He sees the bunker he was to find.

He gets a grenade, pulls out the pin,
A voyage into the unknown,
Blows up the base with him in.
A voyage into death.

Joshua Ainsworth (10)
Banners Gate Junior School

HARRY POTTER

My thoughts are from the tram station.
I want my mom or I'll suck my thumb!
Please Miss Smith open my chocolate bar.
The food tastes horrible, I think my mom left it raw!
It's just like a dream.
Wizards come from the ground, witches' mouldy hands
and maggots too!

My thoughts are from past where the graveyard is.
I feel tired, but I cannot sleep.
Weird things are happening, I'm dizzy,
A witch eating some maggots!
The graveyard is trembling an earthquake is happening!
Hands coming out from the graves!
I want my mom or I'll suck my thumb!

Finally we are there Fin Station.
I'll think of my family all the way, wherever I go.

Andrew Rea (11)
Banners Gate Junior School

I'M AN EVACUEE

I am an evacuee.
I don't have a choice.
Our mother says it's for the best
As she starts to cry.
We love her more than anything
As we do our father.

As I stand on the platform
I hear the train coming
I kiss my mother goodbye
And step onto the train
And as I start to cry
I wave one last wave as the train turns the corner.

We are put into a line
And one by one we are picked
A woman looks at me
She says she'll take me
She looks quite nice
But not like Mother or Father.

This place is quite small
Yet it feels so big.
It's a cottage
It's quite pretty on the outside
There's a big garden outside
It's so different from home.

I started school yesterday
I was scared of them all
They towered over me
The teacher said not to worry
But that was impossible.

I hope the war ends soon.

Natalie Squire (10)
Banners Gate Junior School

EVACUATION

I approach the train, it is red-radish-raw,
The driver presses the button to open up the door,
I wave to my mother,
Then to my brother,
Who is off to fight in the war.

The train leaves,
As I zoom past I see something, a blur in the trees
I think of the bombs,
Then of my mom,
I wonder what will happen in the air, land and seas.

As I come to the station,
I am wondering about the nation,
I think in my head,
Will my mother be dead
When I return from evacuation?

I'm staying in a big house
With Mrs Trouse,
I have my own room,
I'm filled with gloom,
Tears roll down my face.

Mrs Trouse is very kind,
When I misbehave she doesn't mind,
Every day,
She makes me pray,
That none of our men are left behind.

On the wireless the men read out who had been killed in Rome,
I really want to go home,
Luckily my brother hadn't been killed,
Unlike lots of other people in the world,
This thought is always in my head - I want to go home!

Sam Hall (10)
Banners Gate Junior School

JOURNEY TO THE COUNTRY

They're sending me away,
I wonder why
As I sit on the train,
Watching them go by.
Will I ever see them again?
I hope so.

Mom said that a war had started
And Dad was going to war,
Would I ever see him again?
I pray for him more and more,
As I whiz through the station on the train.
I'm going to the country.

Sitting there all on my own,
Where are my mom and dad?
I miss them both very much,
Not being with them makes me sad,
All I'm left with is a photo to touch.
I hope I go to a good home.

Looking out the train,
What can I see?
It looks green and brown,
It could be a tree,
It is nothing like the town.
When will the war end?

Now we are there,
In the countryside.
I miss my mom and dad,
Even though I enjoyed the ride,
I'm still very sad.

Jessica Heath (11)
Banners Gate Junior School

EVACUEE

I was an evacuee
I was taken away
It was bad
It was sad
But most of all it was scary.
All you could see
Was Mr Magee.
The train driver
He was nice
He gave me free rice
It was sweet
With lovely cooked meat.
There was a man
Called Stan
A great guy he was
He died, it's sad
Indeed very bad
He died in the war
A Nazi called Tim
Killed him.
He was horrible
He was like Hitler
Very bitter
Like smelly litter.
I stayed with Adrian
And Dan
His son was Jim
Best friend Tim
But had a broken limb.
I liked my stay.

Jordan Deathridge (10)
Banners Gate Junior School

A Space Poem

Zooming through space I see
Bright stars gleaming,
Buzzing satellites and
A burning sun.

Zooming through space I touch
Huge comets flying,
Spaceships on the ground
And astronauts chattering to each other!

Zooming through space I hear
Green aliens chattering,
Astronauts groaning and
Satellites humming in the air.

Zooming through space I smell
A smoky sun,
Astronauts and green aliens.

Zooming through space I taste
Sugary moondust,
Burning stardust and
Hairy, slimy shooting stardust.

Lucy Idell-Fellows (7)
Banners Gate Junior School

Untitled

Zooming through space I see slimy aliens chatting
Zooming through space I touch huge meteors blasting
Zooming through space I hear shiny satellites buzzing
Zooming through space I smell smoky sun burning.
Zooming through space I taste sugary moondust fizzing.

James Summerfield (8) & Matthew Harris (7)
Banners Gate Junior School

SENSES IN SPACE

Zooming through space . . .
I see stars gleaming,
The fiery sun burning
And the dark aliens jumping.

Zooming through space . . .
I touch huge comets flying,
Silver spaceships floating
And enormous satellites buzzing.

Zooming through space . . .
I hear dark green aliens chatting,
Silver satellites researching
And small stars.

Zooming through space . . .
I smell the burning sun
And the fiery shooting stars.

Zooming through space . . .
I taste the chalky moon
And the moondust . . . yummy!

Georgina Mascoll (8)
Banners Gate Junior School

SAILING THE CARIBBEAN

As I sailed the Caribbean
I saw a star fish
Limping frogs
In the rainforest
Yellow sandy beaches
Shining in the sun.

Daler Turner-Bagot (9)
Banners Gate Junior School

What Can You Smell?

Smell, what can you smell?
I can smell the flowers.
I can smell the dinner.
I can smell the garden.
I can smell the swimming pool.
I can smell the breakfast.
I can smell the apple.
I can smell the pear.
I can smell the orange.
I can smell the banana.
I can smell the barbecue.
I can smell the beach.

Reece Holsey (7)
Banners Gate Junior School

Take Off

I am from out of space
I am an alien
I've travelled for miles and miles
In my rocket.

Counting down to go to Earth
10, 9, 8, 7, 6, 5, 4, 3, 2, 1,
Take off
They are on their way to Earth.

Passing the nine planets
Mercury, Venus, Earth, Mars,
Jupiter, Saturn, Uranus, Neptune, Pluto.

Bradley Taylor (9)
Banners Gate Junior School

Sailing The Caribbean

Sailing the Caribbean Sea
I saw a big, huge whale.
Tall, green, wavy seaweed
Some good, brilliant people swimming.
Scaly, coloured fish swimming through the sea.
A big, huge ferry sailing on the sea.
The shiny, golden shark shining in the sea.
Swaying, green palm trees a dark green colour.
Shiny blue sea reflecting me.
The golden-yellow sun like a fire ball.
Patterned seashells as hard as rock.
The people doing work, getting puffed out.
Tiny, little houses just like stones.

Alex Barr (9)
Banners Gate Junior School

As I Sailed The Caribbean Sea

I saw:-
Green slimy, curly, swaying99
 seaweed.
Shiny, shimmering, scaly, soft fish.
Colourful bright green, beautiful grassy island.
Unique, hairy, swooping, spinning birds
Shining, shimmering, deep blue sea.
Joyful Caribbean
Tiny, peaceful villages,
Amazing crispy orange snapping crabs.
Spiky long tall palm trees.
Big, huge, beeping, sailing cruise liner.
Soft, small green spiky grass.

Luke Fyfe (9)
Banners Gate Junior School

HOLLYWOOD

Look!
What can you see?
Elvis Presley
Rocking and rolling for me.

Look!
(What can you see?)
The shining star
Twinkling for me.

Listen!
(What can you hear?)
The roaring sea
Roaring at me.

Listen!
(What can you hear?)
The Elvis man
Rocking and rolling by the roaring sea.

Touch!
(What can you feel?)
The candyfloss
Skinny and squishy.

Touch!
(What can you feel?)
The old actor's
Squishy chair.

Sniff!
(What can you smell?)
The warm smoke
Of the hot dogs.

Sniff!
(What can you smell?)
The squelchy smell
Of a burger.

Danny Hillman (8)
Banners Gate Junior School

In Spain

Look!
(What can you see?)
The little fish from in the sea
A lovely fish come to me.

Listen!
(What can you hear?)
The roaring sea
And my mom is calling me for my tea.

Touch!
(What can you feel?)
My knife and fork on my plate
And my dad's chalk on the slate.

Sniff!
(What can you smell?)
The lovely smell of the nice burgers
In fact there is no burgers.

Taste!
(What can you taste?)
The lovely taste of chicken nuggets
But you don't need any buckets.

Jonathan Hipkiss (8)
Banners Gate Junior School

Me, An Evacuee

Well goodbye
To my
Mother.
Father's at war.
I'm trying to ignore
The fact that I'm on this train,
Hoping to see them again.

Five hours
To go.
Feeling
Really sick!
Out there it's weird.
All the animals and trees,
All the flowers and bees.

This journey
To a
New home.
These children
From my mansion house
To this place, the countryside.
I tried to stay home, I tried!

I miss home.
I am
Crying.
I'm tired.
It's getting dark.
We're at our destination,
Approaching the train station.
Who's there?
Choose me!
They have.

They look nice.
They live in a pub.
My new life has just begun,
I relax and have some fun.

Kirsty Black (11)
Banners Gate Junior School

ATLANTIC OCEAN

Look!
(What can you see?)
The scaly fish looking at me.

Look!
(What can you see?)
A shining fish going past me.

Listen!
(What can you hear?)
The roaring sea calling to me.

Listen!
(What can you hear?)
A dolphin from a faraway land squeaking to me.

Touch!
(What can you feel?)
A scaly fish going by.

Touch!
(What can you feel?)
The smooth, smooth skin of a dolphin.

Taste!
(What can you taste?)
The salty seawater where the sea creatures are.

Jessica Stevens (7)
Banners Gate Junior School

Journey To A New Home

The train journey
The war had already started,
And bombs were coming down,
I have to go
To the countryside.
The journey to the station
Was really long and hard,
On the steam train
I saw loads of kids.
Wrapped round their shoulders
Stood their gas masks.

Choosing
When we got dropped off,
There were lots of drinks and food,
Can I have one?
That is what I said.
There were lots of men and women
Choosing all of us,
Will I be picked?
I hope it's someone good.
I'll have him.
Then he took me by the hand.
New home
He took me to his house
Which was a little cottage,
It was scary,
He pushed me in the door.

When I was inside
He took my coat off me.
This is quite good,
But I didn't say a word.
I will be all right,
But I miss my mom and dad.

Luke Cragg (10)
Banners Gate Junior School

I'M GOING ON MY BIKE

Look!
(What can you see?)
The curving leaves of a sycamore tree
A shining fish
Looking at me.

Taste!
(What can you taste?)
A chocolate bar and a McDonalds.

Touch!
(What can you taste?)
The hard rock concert
And a nice smooth floor.

Sniff!
(What can you smell?)
The nice clean air
And the smell of an angry bear.

Zak Sheppard (8)
Banners Gate Junior School

Journey To The Countryside

We heard the soldiers coming that morning
We packed our bags and got dressed
'Come on son,' said my dad
I felt scared, I wanted to cry
'It'll be alright if you stay by us,'
We were getting ready to walk out of the house for the last time.

We walked out of the front door for the last time
You could see other people setting off too just like us.
Some people I knew and some I didn't
There were people as far as the eye could see
I felt really scared.

It was half way through our journey
We were alright so far
But what's that noise? *Bang! Bang!* and talking
He and a couple of other people hid in the woods
Luckily they passed us
But some people weren't so lucky.

We stopped there until about 9.30
Then we set off
That night it was spooky and wind in the forest
The wind howled like a wolf
It was like a scene from a horror film
It was the most spooky day of my life.

I was very excited and also tired
Everyone was talking about it
I was just about to have a drink
When someone shouted, 'There is it,'
Everyone looked
We ran that last mile
We finally made it.

Steven Todd (11)
Banners Gate Junior School

Being A War Evacuee

I left behind me a dull, bleak city,
To come to the beautiful countryside.
At the station I said goodbye to Mom.
I was all dirty, my shorts were a rag.
While dragging behind my rugged old bag
With the objects inside packed especially for me,
I got on the train, my old bag and me.

I'm on a big train
Seeing many different sights,
Far away from the bright city lights.
My journey so far is getting exciting,
Much different now from the war and fighting.
I wonder what adventures await me,
Just hoping that they shall be glee.

On my arrival the family were waiting
To greet me and show me my new home.
On my way home they were all so nice to me,
Including my brother and sister,
Danny and Bea.
The cottage they lived in was so big and tall,
And a garden with roses and trees.

Today I went to my new school,
But was bullied by a gang of boys.
Then Danny came up and saved me.
The next day I was off school ill,
I wrote to my mother a letter,
She wrote one back saying 'Get better.'

Two years later I'm back in London
With my mom and the war is over.

Tara Rowe (11)
Banners Gate Junior School

THE EXPERIENCE OF AN EVACUEE

I wait on the platform
As Mum waves goodbye,
I comfort my sister
As she starts to cry.

I enter the carriage
As it starts to rain
And tears run down my face
As we wave goodbye again.

As the train moves on,
The city disappears
And I sit back
And wipe away my tears.

Woods and fields
Are speeding past,
As we reach the countryside
At last.

The billeting officer took us
To the village hall.
The man that picked us
Was big and tall.

The man was so tall,
I felt as small; as a mouse,
As we stepped into the Land Rover,
And headed for his house.

The man that picked us
Lived on a farm,
And I soon learnt that the animals
Would do me no harm.

Is there an end
To this stress and sorrow?
Is there going to be
A tomorrow?

Kelly Draper (10)
Banners Gate Junior School

USA

Look!
(What can you see?)
The front of a sting ray coming closer to me.
A distant boat throwing waves in the sea.

Listen!
(What can you hear?)
A big sea roaring at me.
The great big noise of people screaming at the sea.

Sniff!
(What can you smell?)
The hot, hot smell of hot dog.
A great big smell of a hot cooking pot.

Touch!
(What can you feel?)
The little duckling with fluffy fur.
A little sheep going 'Baa! Baa!'

Taste!
(What can you taste?)
The slippery skin of a ripe banana.
A fish that tastes like a piranha.

Ryan Willis (7)
Banners Gate Junior School

Evacuee Poem

I am feeling sad,
So really sad,
I'm leaving home,
I feel so bad.

Because of the war,
They're sending me,
Into the country,
For my safety.

At a half past nine,
I'm due on the train,
We walk up the road,
It starts to rain.

My mom is crying,
My dad is glum,
I'm not happy,
I've a pain in my tum.

I step on the train,
My head hanging low,
I look out the window,
As the train starts to go.

My dad is waving,
My mom is too,
We try a smile,
But it's hard to do.

The journey is long,
And tiring to me,
We at last arrive,
At half past three.

We go round houses,
Hoping to be chosen,
We stand at the door,
Of Mr and Mrs Rosen.

She looks at us all,
And smiles with glee,
She looks rather nice,
I hope she picks me.

I go inside,
With my little case,
I look around,
At my new base.

I'm so pleased,
That they've picked me,
I get unpacked,
And we have tea.

I've been here ages,
The Rosens are nice,
My mom and dad are fine,
I've heard from them twice.

Zoe Barrow (10)
Banners Gate Junior School

THE POETIC VOYAGE

When we went to the moon I heard a tune
The stars were sparkling by Mars
I saw the sun and shot it with a gun
When we went to Jupiter my brother lost my mother
Then we landed on Mars with flowers and jars
My baby sister thought the sun was fun.

Ashley Hillier (9)
Banners Gate Junior School

SANDY BEACH

Look!
(What can you see?)
The beautiful sandy beach
Of a palm tree.
The shells on the sand
Of a weeping willow.

Listen!
(What can you hear?)
The kind children playing
Of a parent calling.
The ice cream van
Of a kind man calling.
The singing children of a mother like I.

Touch!
(What can you feel?)
The shiny shells
Of a stony beach.
The blue dolphin
Of a river high.

Taste!
(What can you taste?)
The ice cream strawberry
Of a summer day.
The salty sea
Of a distant bay.

Sniff!
(What can you smell?)
The horrible fish
Of a fishmonger.
The chlorine
Of a gentle swimming bath calming.

Charlotte Taylor (8)
Banners Gate Junior School

WATER WORLD

Look!
(What can you see?)
The very large fin of a great white shark,
The lights of a boat shining in the dark.

Listen!
(What can you hear?)
The splash and roar of the crashing waves,
The sun above on the first of May.

Touch!
(What can you feel?)
The hard, brittle sticks of a lump of coral,
The little tiny hole of a sand worm's burrow.

Sniff!
(What can you smell?)
The musty smell of floating seaweed,
The man on the beach eating green cheese.

Taste!
(What can you taste?)
The tiny grains of the sour salt,
The smell of chips on a boat's hull.

Lucy Ford (7)
Banners Gate Junior School

On My Way To The Isle Of Man

Look!
(What can you see?)
I can see the sea looking at me
And I can see the birds flying over me.

Touch!
(What can you feel?)
I can feel the waves splashing
At me.

Sniff!
(What can you smell?)
I can smell the seafood
Waiting for me.

Taste!
(What can you taste?)
I can taste the sea
Calling for me.

Listen!
(What can you hear?)
I can hear the waves
Calling to me.

Lucy Ashcroft (7)
Banners Gate Junior School

Deep, Deep Down In The Sea

Deep, deep down in the sea,
It's nice and relaxing,
It's really soft and calm,
I see all the little fish as I pass them,
As I pass the fish I see all kinds of ships.

Deep, deep down in the sea,
I sail through the big calm ocean,
I see this shark,
I am terrified,
It is massive,
But it passes me, phew!

Claire Lee (9)
Banners Gate Junior School

Campsite At A Wildlife Park

Look!
What can you see?
The winds and the rain
Crashing together.

Listen!
What can you hear?
The snapping
Of a crocodile at me
The crinkling and crackling
Of the leaves on the tree.

Touch!
What can you feel?
The prickly touch
Of a berry bush
The silky fur
Of a nice old thrush.

Paul Bird (7)
Banners Gate Junior School

THE SEA THAT COMES TO ME

Look!
(What can you see?)
The crashing waves
Of a white bit of foam
A windy howl of the roaring sea
And there it is because it can see me.

Listen!
(What can you hear?)
The distant tree near by me
Of a magpie coming to me
A cage next to me
I open it to let the poor thing free.

Touch!
(What can you feel?)
The sprinkly sand
Of a big, big land
A hairy monster and I'm in his hand!
I jump out of his hand
And then I'm back on the land.

Sniff!
(What can you smell?)
The happiness of wetness
Of a fish swimming by
A shark having fun
Of a man having a bun
And a boy saying 'Bye-bye.'

Taste!
(What can you taste?)
The smell of chips
Coming to me
Of a yellow sand and salt
And there I am
Choking on lots of sand
From in my hand!

Theresa Matthews (7)
Banners Gate Junior School

SPACE

Zooming through space I see . . .
Shiny solar systems shining,
Humming satellites buzzing,
Slimy aliens fighting.

Zooming through space I touch . . .
Crystal planets clear,
Shooting comets gleaming,
Shiny shooting stars flying.

Zooming through space I hear . . .
Bleepy satellites bleeping,
Slimy aliens groaning.

Zooming through space I smell . . .
Smoky sun burning.

Zooming through space I taste . . .
Sparkly moondust fizzing.

Jake Riley (7)
Banners Gate Junior School

HOLLYWOOD USA

Look!
(What can you see?)
The little light so very bright
Of a shining star to light up
The dark, dark forest on
The light, light night.

Touch!
(What can you feel?)
The spiky old starfish
And a small old dish
The smooth nice skin
Of a spiky pin.

Taste!
(What can you taste?)
The juicy tasty fish
As I plop it in my dish
The nice hot dog
Of a great big dog.

Sniff!
(What can you smell?)
The great big yolk
And a big, big smoke.

Listen!
(What can you hear?)
The roaring howl of the sea
A little fish looks at me
As the wailing wind
Of a cod all tinned.

Jesse Gordon (8)
Banners Gate Junior School

AT THE SEA

Look!
(What can you see?)
The splashing waves
Of a crashing sea.
A big fish coming up to me.

Listen!
(What can you hear?)
The seagulls flying up
In the air
They are making a squawking noise.

Touch!
(What can you feel?)
The feel of a cold sea
And the little waves
Splashing on my wrist.

Sniff!
(What can you smell?)
The smell of the fresh air
And the smell of salt
From the sea.

Taste!
(What can you taste?)
The taste of
A melting ice cream
Of a twister.

Arran Thompson (7)
Banners Gate Junior School

EVACUATED

Waiting for the train,
Time passing by,
Children crying,
Bags in hands,
Wave goodbye.

Going to the countryside,
Sitting in my seat,
Children sobbing,
Wheels rolling,
Take us away.

Here we are at the station,
Jumping off the steps,
Crowds of children,
Standing small,
Ladies calling names.

Standing tall and straight,
In a giant hall,
Adults everywhere,
Taking children home,
It's my turn.

Walking out of the hall,
A lady clutching my arm,
People staring,
At all the kids,
Wondering what their new homes are like.

On the way home,
Glad the war's over,
Children smiling,
Eating food,
Ready to get home.

Oliver Wadhams (10)
Banners Gate Junior School

Skiathos!

Look!
(What can you see?)
Me looking in the mirror
Looking at me
Getting ready to go out
To have my tea.

Listen!
(What can you hear?)
The crickets screeching
Their wings at night
While fireflies show their
Big bright light.

Touch!
(What can you feel?)
Soft smooth sand
On the sandy beach
Hard rock pebbles
On the dusty land.

Taste!
(What can you taste?)
The lovely melting ice cream
Melting in my mouth
The salty sand in my tummy
Which goes tingling too.

Sniff!
(What can you smell?)
The fish cooking on the stove
Lucky for me I'm not those,
Or I'll be dead
I would rather eat bread.

Paige Chattaway (8)
Banners Gate Junior School

JOHN'S CABIN LOG

Look!
(What can you hear?)
The big high hump
Of a mouse not light,
A shining star,
Of course it's bright.

Listen!
(What can you hear?)
The great big crunch
Of a crooked old leaf,
A roaring fire
Cooking the beef.

Touch!
(What can you feel?)
The algae great bark
Of a massive tree,
A tiny grasshopper
Looking at me.

Sniff!
(What can you smell?)
The fresh clean air
Of a big high breeze,
A lump of dirt
Sitting on my knees.

Taste!
(What can you taste?)
The orange spaghetti
On my tongue,
A refreshing air
In my lung.

Andrew Cotterill (8)
Banners Gate Junior School

Germany

Look!
(What can you see?)
A tree looking at me
The axe cutting me
A black axe you see
And not an ordinary tree.

Listen!
(What can you hear?)
The wind blowing over a sycamore tree
Not an ordinary sycamore tree
A brown sycamore tree.

Taste!
(What can you taste?)
Fruit melting in my mouth
As the sweet taste comes out
And I taste it myself.

Touch!
(What can you feel?)
The water flood on a road
And a lot for the mud car road.

Sniff!
(What can you sniff?)
The nice smell
The nice taste
And the stink of the horrid smell.

Bradley Byrne (7)
Banners Gate Junior School

DISNEYLAND

Look!
(What can you see?)
The bolts on the floor
Then more
The castle is small
And a big ball.

Listen!
(What can you hear?)
Noise
And more noise
Noises.

Touch!
(What can you feel?)
The toils of a mermaid's tail
And the bunch of mail.

Sniff!
(What can you smell?)
The cold fresh air
And the smell of a greedy bear.

Taste!
(What can you taste?)
A jar of malt
And mouldy salt.

Marie Williams (8)
Banners Gate Junior School

At The Caribbean

Look!
(What can you see?)
The crashing waves looking at me
Of a white light looking at me.

Listen!
(What can you hear?)
The far away calling to me
Of a big distant sea waving to me.

Touch!
(What can you feel?)
The fish kissing me
Of a golden fish loving me.

Sniff!
(What can you smell?)
The warm tomato soup on the desk
Of a lovely brown poodle calling to me
In the pet shop.

Taste!
(What can you taste?)
The cold coconut drink
Of a lovely bright sun.

Thomas Price (8)
Banners Gate Junior School

EVACUATED

My mum and I are walking towards the train hand in hand,
All ages of children are standing on this land,
My suitcases are being loaded as I start to cry,
My mom grips my hand tightly and I wonder why,
I can hear screaming and shouting as children are dragged away,
I hope we will be able to come back someday.

'You have to go now,' my mom whispers in my ear,
All of a sudden I start to feel queer,
My mom kisses me on my head and pushes me on the train,
I turn around and look at her; has she gone insane?
My heartbeat is very fast and my eyes are full of tears,
Screams, shouts and cries are what fill my ears.

Out of the window I see bushes and trees, it is very vast,
How long will this journey last?
Children are all moaning, not laughing but crying,
On the train it sounds like we're all dying,
Brothers and sisters are holding on to each other,
Everybody is crying, 'I want my mother!'

The train comes to a halt and everything is still,
The doors are opening but in comes no chill,
Outside are farmers' meadows and hills,
Also sheep and cows and lots of mills,
As we step out from the train there are lots of 'Aahs' and 'Oohs',
'Right everybody now it's time to choose.'

People, people everywhere,
Who I go to I don't care,
All I want is to go back home,
Then I won't feel so alone,
Please don't choose me, pass me by,
Then I can get on the train and say bye-bye.

Dawn Wakefield (10)
Banners Gate Junior School

When I Knew I Was Going To Be Evacuated?

I didn't know what to say and the next day I had to get on the train.
I had to take my gas mask and my bag with a chocolate bar inside.
Plus my belongings. The journey was a very long ride
but I'm okay and I am very hot. My new family are very nice to me
and I have got a younger brother, his name is Tom.
It is scary in the city but there is no bombing going on here.
I wonder if Dad is alive? He's fighting in the war.

Anyway, how are you? Are you scared?
I am missing you and Dad. Has there been any more sirens yet?
If a siren goes off we all have to go under the train station because
it is very safe down there.

The Germans never bombed the countryside before.
On the way here I saw the most beautiful animals you could
ever see in your life. They were all sorts of different colours.

James Baker (10)
Banners Gate Junior School

Zooming Through Space

Zooming through space I see a bright shooting star
with sparks coming out.
Zooming through space I touch the planet Pluto and it feels quite funny.
Zooming through space I hear aliens groaning, shooting in space.
Zooming through space I smell the sun, burning hot, not very nice.
Zooming through space I taste the dust, it is lovely.

Jessica Hill (7)
Banners Gate Junior School

As I Sailed The Caribbean I Saw

Flowing, swaying seaweed
In the bottom of the sea
Strange, dead shells
Beautiful and wonderful
Bright surfing water
The waves are coming
Multicoloured, beautiful fish
Fat, big, thin and small and all kinds
Fantastic, wonderful birds
Flying in mid air like an angel
Wonderful, pretty people
Having a lot of fun
Rough, giant palm trees
Growing yummy coconuts
Slippy, smooth sand
Waiting to play with you and me
Small grounded villages
That people want to go and get!

Sian Frater (8)
Banners Gate Junior School

Walking

Walking, walking, what a pain
All you do is sit down again
What's the point, I can't get to grips
With the long, long dreary trips
Some people walk with their legs right apart
Some people walk, coming straight from the heart
Once you start going you eventually stop
I just can't get it so now I just *hop!*

Josh Taylor (11)
Lindens JMI School

NORMAN'S WAND

When old Pete came out of the bin
Everyone said he smelt again.
Norman got out his magic wand
And began to walk towards the pond.

Then poor Pete went to the pond
And there he saw a magic wand.
Norman stepped in front of him
And kicked him quite hard in the shin.

Pete walked off and then he froze,
He thought someone was spraying him with a hose.
It was really Norman's wand,
It wasn't coming from the pond.
Then poor Pete began to run
It was no use, he was under his spell.

Matthew Folan (10)
Lindens JMI School

CHRISTMAS

Christmas comes once a year,
Holidays are nearly here,
Reach for the stars that are high,
Imagine that you're going to fly,
Santa riding through the snow,
Trains are going very slow,
Modelling around the Christmas tree,
Adults wrapping presents as you can see,
Snowflakes coming from high,
So that's the end, I will say goodbye.

Abbie Hodson (10)
Lindens JMI School

MY RABBIT PATCH

My rabbit loves to eat
Crushed cereal and Shredded Wheat,
When he's hungry he'll nibble his feet,
But I love Patch.
In the morning he loves to play,
In the night he sleeps in hay,
One time, he slept all day!
But I love Patch.
His big eyes are sky blue,
When I go upstairs he'll follow me to the loo!
Does he like me? Don't have a clue!
But I love Patch.
He'll run up and down the lumpy stairs,
Sometimes losing his long black hairs,
His favourite dessert is chopped pears,
But I love Patch!

Laraib Rana (10)
Lindens JMI School

THE OLD STEAM TRAIN

The old steam train creaked along
Back to the station where it belonged
Steam rose high
Passed the stream which now stood dry

Long tall grasses and dells
Passed trees and pretty bluebells
Through the tunnel, black as night
It rumbled out to the light

The paint was dirty from the smoke
Tables and chairs now were broke
The happy days it had seen
Were nothing more than a dream

The train neared the end of the line
It was old now and out of time
Through the station it was led
Then retired happily to its shed.

Robert Smith (11)
Lindens JMI School

SISTER, SISTER

Sister, sister come over here
Sister, sister happy new year!
Sister, sister you're really boring
Sister, sister you are always drawing.

Sister, sister don't do that
Sister, sister wipe your feet on the mat.
Sister, sister please play a game
Sister, sister you are always the same!

Sister, sister Mia's your name
Sister, sister you play girls' games.
Sister, sister you dress really silly
Sister, sister I wish you were called Billy.

Sister, sister please don't cry
Sister, sister you know I lie!

Matthew Bates (10)
Lindens JMI School

My Friends And School

School, school, it's not that cool
School, school, it's got a big pool.

My friend Sam,
He got a cool tan.
My cousin Darren,
Wants to be like Aaron.
Some girl called Diane
Is going out with Ryan.

School, school, it's not that cool,
School, school, it's got a rule.
Don't run in the hall!
Please be quiet all!

Craig Pedley (10)
Lindens JMI School

Cats! Cats!

Cats, cats, they hiss and they scratch
They like eating things, especially rats.
They run like mad and fight each other
They get on your nerves just like their mother.

Cats, cats, they like dangly things
They like chasing birds with colourful wings
They scrounge for food and nice soft toys
They pick on people, especially boys.

Cats, cats, they snuggle and purr
Their coats are warm of fine thick fur
They're not so bad on an overall
But the problem is they don't come when you call.

Oliver Williams (11)
Lindens JMI School

ORANG-UTANS

I love to watch the orang-utans
Swinging in the tree.

I love to watch the orang-utans
Staring back at me.

I love to watch the orang-utans
Munching on their fruit.

I love to watch the orang-utans
They are so cuddly and cute.

I love to watch the orang-utans
Playing with their mates.

I love to watch the orang-utans
Because they are so great.

I love to watch the orang-utans
They are so beautiful to see.

I love to watch the orang-utans
It's just a shame they are in captivity.

Rachel Acton (10)
Lindens JMI School

GLOBAL WARMING RAP

Global warming, it's not funny,
It makes the polar ice caps runny.

Those car engines really stink,
They're starting to make islands sink.

Industrialists really don't care,
All they wanna do is pollute the air.

Holes over here, holes over there,
Look at the state of the ozone layer.

Our homes will be floating in the sea,
Then we're just gonna say, 'Oh dear me.'

Here's a clue what to do,
To stop Mother Earth getting the flu,
Recycle everything that you can,
And stop driving any sort of van.

James Byrne (10)
Lindens JMI School

ALIENS

Aliens are green and slimy with purple spots,
They live on Mars and do alien dot to dots.
Some aliens work at alien coffee shops,
But most work at offices making blue bottle tops.

Alien kings and queens sit on orange goo,
Alien teachers there's nothing new.
Aliens eat burgers and mouldy chips,
And live in huts that are total tips.

Cheese is the moon-monster's favourite food,
Martians are really very rude.
Aliens are the very best,
If I had to decide they would beat the rest.

Lauren Davies (10)
Lindens JMI School

Hamster's World

Hamsters act in different ways,
But they won't perform in plays.
Some are really very furry,
And won't act one bit girly.

They will bite,
Not fly a kite.
They will gnaw,
Walk on the floor.

They will eat up all their food,
And walk around almost nude.
They are very, very small,
And will not grow one bit tall.

They will go on their wheel,
But they won't eat orange peel.
They will live in our house,
And as quiet as a mouse.

Nathan Worton (11)
Lindens JMI School

My Favourite Author

Jacqueline Wilson's my favourite author,
Bad Girls and Monster Story Teller,
Check out Alex in How To Survive Summer Camp,
Make time to read Double Act,
You'll be hooked, that's a fact.

Lucy Bradbury (10)
Lindens JMI School

My Pet Dog

I've got a dog,
small and black,
Tally the name,
'*Cats*' I say, then she runs,
pulling me behind her.

Aimee demonte (10)
Lindens JMI School

Blue

Blue is the colour of my room,
like the music that is zoom,
usually I play on my computer,
end your playing on your scooter.

Aimee Shingler (11)
Lindens JMI School

DINOSAURS

Dinosaurs, dinosaurs
Big types, small types
Thin types, fat types
Some as long as very big pipes

They live in trees
They live on the ground
They fly in the air
Without any sound

They eat plants
They eat each other
They eat fish
They sometimes eat their mother

They used to fly
They used to hide
Then something happened
And they died!

Thomas Walker (10)
Lindens JMI School

WHO AM I?

I am big and strong.
Golden with spots.
I've got a very long neck.
I live in the African jungle.

What am I?
A giraffe.

Ryan Edwards (11)
Lindens JMI School

I Hate The Rain

I hate the rain, it makes life boring.
Especially in the house where Dad is snoring,
I hate the rain because you can't play outside,
As soon as it stops I'll be happy, and it will have dried,
Just think what I could do once the rain has gone,
I could play on my bike or even play with John,
Rain, rain please go away,
Because if you don't it will be boring all day.

I was watching the weather,
After 'Birds Of A Feather',
To see if it said anything about our rain,
But it didn't, so I wrote to complain,
Come the next day,
It said the rain would go away,
I thought that the weather man was just telling lies,
But when I woke up in the morning I couldn't believe my eyes.

Paul Keepax (10)
Lindens JMI School

About School Food

The food at my school is sick,
and so says my friend Benjamin Nick.
Mushy peas and baked beans too,
they make me go to the loo.
Chips and hot dogs, they're the best,
except for chocolate cake (it's better than the rest).
Now let's get it straight, there's nothing more sick
than school food!

Kamendeep Singh Gill (11)
Lindens JMI School

A Wild Football Match

Football is a wild game,
It's never the same.
As I go running down the line,
Waiting to pass to my friend Albertine.
The crowd goes wild,
As the ball hits a child.
The mother of the child,
Goes completely wild,
Running from side to side.
All the players stop to watch,
The mother going completely wild.
It takes a while to calm her down,
Like I say football can be a wild game.

Alyson Hunt (11)
Lindens JMI School

My Rabbit Rosie

My rabbit Rosie loves to sit around all day,
But sometimes comes inside to play.
When I go to feed her every morning,
She always comes up to me yawning.
I love to watch Rosie,
In the night getting all cosy.
I bet you she dreams about being a knight,
And sometimes after flying a kite.
But she knows when she wakes up in the morning
She'll be Rosie again.

Rebecca Stanford (10)
Lindens JMI School

A SNOWY SUNDAY

Snow, snow everywhere
I jumped out of bed, what shall I wear?
Pants and socks
Lots and lots
A T-shirt and a jumper.

Waterproof trousers
A coat, a hat
And a pair of gloves
With a woolly scarf
Which made my mom laugh

I am ready to go
And play in the snow
Oh, I am a nelly, I forgot my welly!

Ryan Page (10)
Lindens JMI School

SATS TEST

SATs test, SATs test, I really hate SATs test,
SATs test, SATs test, they take up my time,
SATs test, SATs test, they are a testing time,
I think I would rather be resting,
That would be fine!
SATs test, SATs test, however they have to be done!
So the quicker I get them over,
The more time I will have for fun.
SATs test, SATs test, so I hope to do well,
SATs test, SATs test, will bring out my best.

Joseph Carlon (11)
Lindens JMI School

THE TEST

To start the test I put my name
It seemed like I was playing a game,
I opened the paper to see
That the questions were too hard for me.

As the teacher was explaining
I noticed that it was raining,
As the test was about to start
I put my hand upon my heart.

I noticed it was beating fast
Then I realised I would be last,
I don't know! Copy from a friend,
Help me, help me, when will this end.

Laura Syner (11)
Lindens JMI School

WHO AM I?

I am big and strong,
I'm also quiet,
My brain is as good as a human's,
I am quick as light.
Who am I?

I can kill,
I can catch my food,
I live in the grassy plains,
I am the king of the jungle.
Who am I?

Wilson Tang (10)
Lindens JMI School

THE WEAKEST LINK

Anne Robinson makes people want to cry,
She says 'You are the weakest link, goodbye!'
She says this to every woman and man,
It is such an abusive programme.

If there's a tie, the strongest link
Has to choose and has to think
Which one he would like to go
The weakest link then feels quite low.

Thank goodness I'm not on that show
The weakest link just has to go,
They call her the mistress in black,
At the end of each show, she says, 'I'll be back!'

Neil Coleman (11)
Lindens JMI School

ANDY PANDY

Andy Pandy is a nice lad
He always takes a note book pad
He also likes sleeping
And you know he likes eating

Andy Pandy
Likes candy
He got fatter and fatter
Soon he pops
And then I put him in the box
And that was the end of Andy Pandy.

Andrew Reilly (10)
Lindens JMI School

DISCO, DISCO

Disco, disco have a dance
Sometimes there is a lot of romance
Come along and have some fun
Will accept just one chum

Dress up nice, you can pull anyone
Nice ones, weird ones, just pick one
Some of them are like Celine Dion

We're buzzing along having a great time
She said to me, 'Do you want to dine?'
I said to her 'Any time.'
Five hours later she phoned me up
She spoke to me and said, 'Wwwaaazzzuuuppp!'

Ben Jones (10)
Lindens JMI School

CHRISTMAS

Christmas only comes once a year,
Holidays are really near,
Relax it's Christmas, put up your tree,
Igloos being made without a key,
Sledges sliding in the snow,
Trees being cut very low,
Mistletoe hung where you can see,
Any people will kiss to be,
So merry Christmas and goodbye from me.

Ellie Forouhandeh (10)
Lindens JMI School

Spaceman

You are on Mars
With no space cars
No petrol or fuel,
That's really cool!

Jupiter is a step away
With lots of room to stand and sway
Spaceman you are the best
You got there first and beat the rest.

You are on the moon
You'll come back soon
Other spacemen shout and bellow
As you come down, just say 'Hello.'

You've been on Mars, you've been on the moon,
Who knows where you will go soon
Spaceman you are the best
You got there first and beat the rest.

Robert Bishop (11)
Lindens JMI School

My Animal

My animal is gold
and has a body of silk.
My animal is cold blooded
and he likes to swim.
My animal has got fins of silver and gold.
My animal is young yet very old.
My animal is a goldfish.

Jonathan Leafe (10)
Lindens JMI School

Zoo

Yesterday I went to the zoo,
I saw a monkey and kangaroo,
The snake was scary,
The bear very hairy,
And the tiger roared from his den.

Yesterday I went to the zoo,
I saw a panda eating bamboo,
The seals splashed,
While the lion dashed,
And the elephant waved his trunk.

Yesterday I went to the zoo,
I saw a leopard and rhino too,
The giraffe was tall,
While the rabbit was small,
Oh what fun is the zoo.

Emma Harrison (10)
Lindens JMI School

Friends

Friends, friends are always there,
Friends, friends always care.
Friends laugh, friends cry,
Friends say hi and bye.
Friends play games,
Friends stick together.
Friends, best friends,
Friends stay friends forever!

Aisha Zentani (10)
Lindens JMI School

My Best Friend From Mars

My best friend from Mars
Has three coloured eyes and six arms
He has one head and four feet
And is rounded with flubber and meat

My best friend called Joge
Is really quite good at jokes
He's good at modelling dough
And enjoys sucking his toes
He's the hippiest hoppiest guy alive
In the hippiest happiest way

'Cause my best friend from Mars
Has three coloured eyes and six arms
He has one head and four feet
And is rounded with flubber and meat

My best friend is my best chum
And will always be
'Cause we stick together
Like blood bro's forever
And nothing will detach thee

'Cause my best friend from Mars
Has three coloured eyes and six arms
He has one head and four feet
And is rounded with flubber and meat.

Thomas Hull (10)
Lindens JMI School

Cats Act

Cats act in all different ways,
Some sit on window bays.
Some like to scratch,
Some will find their match.
Some will climb
At any time.

Cats act in all sporting ways,
Sometimes they'll rise.
Cats like running away,
Some miaow, hooray.
Some will bring in the house,
A small mouse.

Cats even take you by surprise,
Sometimes they get more exercise
Than you think.
Lots of milk they drink.
They eat a mouse
In the house.

Cats are different colours.
Brown, black and even white.
Sometimes they'll even bite.
They sleep at night,
Awake when it is bright.
Cats cause all kinds of blunders.

James Dudley (10)
Lindens JMI School

SPORTS

Sports, sports, you win and you lose
Sometimes you get cheers and sometimes booze
Football and tennis they both use a ball
Polo and swimming you play in a pool.

Sports, sports, girls and boys play
Man U are winning in the FA
Rounders and baseball, both sports use a bat
Golfing and cricket they always wear hats.

Sports, sports, keep healthy and fit
For all of these sports you need your kit
You'll be sorry if you can't run
All you'll be eating is an ice cream bun.

Ben Clougher (11)
Lindens JMI School

WE BROKE FRIENDS TODAY

We broke friends today
Me and my friend Faye.
We used to be the best of friends
Our friendship now will never mend.

We go our separate ways
Long hours, long days.
Pass through my endless life
Without my best friend Faye.

I wish I could be best friends with Faye
I want to make friends, now, today.
I don't care what it takes
I trip to the zoo, a plate full of cakes.

We made friends in the end
She said she was sorry, so did I.
But then she was horrible, so I was too
But the bad news is
We broke friends again!

Laura Richards (11)
The Shrubbery School

CREATURES

As I walk through the night
Owls lurk on the top branches of trees
Maybe creatures are looking at me
I shiver in fear
Then out jumps a cat
The fiend made me fall over!

I carry on down the path
I see branches move in the trees
Could it be the wind or creatures
Watching me in the night?
I start to move faster
Then all of a sudden a dog jumps behind me barking
It starts to chase me
I run down the garden path with my heart pounding
Open the door and then bang the door shut
I'm relieved and I'm safe.

Charles Stanley (10)
The Shrubbery School

My Dad

I have a dad
He's a very bossy dad
And he often likes to show me up
He wakes up every morning
From the sound of his own snoring
And he drinks his morning tea in a red cup.

I have a dad
He's a very helpful dad
And he helps me when my homework is so hard
He helps me with my motorbike
Which always stalls with a sudden strike
And we play exciting games in the back yard.

I have a dad
He's a very comforting dad
And he comforts me when I'm in an awful mood
He drives very speedily
And gets drunk very easily
And he likes to spend his spare time eating food.

Ashwin Roy (11)
The Shrubbery School

Rainbow

Red is the colour in children's faces,
Orange is the sun that sets in different places,
Yellow is the sun high in the sky,
Green is the grass as you pass by,
Blue is the sea that shines from the sun,
Indigo is the plum that makes you have some fun,
Violet is the last colour of the rainbow.

Red is the colour of blood,
Orange is the lava that comes from a volcano,
Yellow is the skin of a dead fish,
Green is the colour of terrible jealousy,
Blue is the colour of beaten-up children,
Indigo is the dark sky and the time thieves come out,
Violet is the colour of terrible hatred.

Dominique Reid (11)
The Shrubbery School

LEO

Leo is my little dog
His whiskers are like silver spaghetti
He's very small and cute
He jumps up at everything and then
Woof, woof, woof, the door bell goes
Leo goes mad, *oh no!*

Leo's salt and pepper fur is coarse
And prickly like a porcupine
He looks at other dogs like terriers
And says 'Growwwl'.

He loves his basket - he sometimes won't leave
The only way he gets out is if he sees the little silver dish
Which means food! Food!
He's due for a clip, his hair is getting long
But will he like it? No!

He's a show dog who has won one gold medal
He loves to eat anything but won't sit down
But he will always be mine, Leo my Schnauzer.

Matthew O'Hara (10)
The Shrubbery School

This Little Itch

I have this little itch
That bothers me all the time,
I have this little itch
Oh, it's so hard to rhyme.

I have this little itch,
I get it every day,
I have this little itch
And it won't go away.

I have this little itch
And it's always on my heel,
I have this little itch,
My skin's begun to peel.

I have this little itch,
It always annoys me,
I have this little itch,
I'd rather be stung by a bee!

I have this little itch,
But what I am trying to say,
I have this little itch,
And it won't go away!

William Murcott (11)
The Shrubbery School

Bob My Special Friend

Bob my special friend,
It is a shame he's only a puppet.

Who sits upon my shelf,
I stare at him from my bed,
Gazing at his ginger head.
He dresses like a punk,
With his chains and trendy trainers.

When I take him to school
Everyone thinks he's so cool,
That's my special budding
Friend called Bob!

Graham Cadman (11)
The Shrubbery School

THE ROBBERS

One night whilst I was sleeping
Robbers came and prowled
They crept downstairs
And burst into our lounge
First they took the video
Then the DVD

When I came down in the morning
Nothing was there to see
My mum called the police
It was such a surprise
We could hardly believe our eyes
The police said 'Don't worry
We will be right over.'

They inspected the house saying
Nothing was to be seen
Not even any evidence
Everything was clean.

So they gave up looking for
This criminal and said
'Get an alarm for your property
Or you'll have burglars instead.'

Rana Alam (9)
The Shrubbery School

Tiger

Tiger, long, orange, black
Hiding behind a big tree dark
Slickly walking in the grass
Four fast legs, always late for class
It can tear a hundred little cars
It can run as fast as anything
It can catch a gazelle with just one spring
Tears off the meat and tucks it away
Into the sand or the snow goes its prey
Then it's out to play and sleep all day
Hunted human beings, ate them for his tea
One of them was an Eskimo
One of them had his clothes on
Another had a hat to chew on
And finally *help,* it's me!

Jamie Ingram (9)
The Shrubbery School

Mountains

Clouds that hang like thick snow across the peak,
The summit pointing to the sun,
Still attractive it stands proudly above the earth,
Soldier-like but beautiful,
Watching over the village.

Protecting it from terrorising winds,
Marauding from the north,
Soldier-like but beautiful,
Watching over the village.

Securing the village from the moors,
Keeping nature far away,
Soldier-like but beautiful,
Watching over the village.

Charlotte Bartram (11)
The Shrubbery School

DREAMS

Dreams can be sunny
Dreams can be funny
Dreams can be mad
Dreams can be sad
Dreams can make you glad.

Dreams can make you joyful
Dreams can be colourful
Dreams can be crafty
Dreams can be dafty
Dreams are 'dreams'.

In your dreams you can be flying
You can be dying
You can be chasing
You can be fainting
Dreams are dreams.

You can be in a greedy dream
You can be in a racing team
You can be in a mean dream
You can be in a dream where you are mean
Dreams are dreams.

Emily Turner (8)
The Shrubbery School

Friend Poem

My friend cries like a tap still running
as soon as she starts she never stops. *Dominique.*

My friend is right as rain
but when she grazes her knee she is right down again. *Jessica.*

My friend is like a piggy and squeals
to get her own way with things. *Sara.*

My friend's hair is so sharp like darts
she is so hard to miss because she is as tall as a skyscraper. *Kelly.*

My friend is like a lolly
when you tell her a joke she goes all jolly. *Laura.*

My friend is like the sunshine.
In the sun her hair is white. *Alice.*

Hannah Stafford (10)
The Shrubbery School

Badgers

Badgers are amazing creatures,
They have many wondrous features,
A little grey nose, with a good sense of smell,
Black and white fur, which they clean very well,
Ivory teeth as sharp as butcher's knives,
Silvery whiskers which last them their lives.

Badgers hunt in the middle of the night,
Enough to give any dormouse a fright,
Prowling around looking for prey,
Smaller creatures try to hide away,
But the badger picks up the scent of meat,
An evening's dinner for him to eat.

Badgers are so very shy,
They hide away from prying eyes,
If humans try to get too near,
The badger will just disappear,
Deep down into its cosy sett,
Where all its creature comforts met.

Christopher Ferguson (11)
The Shrubbery School

My Cat

My cat is ferocious,
Just like a lion,
With her sharp claws
And her big growl!

How she prowls for mice and voles,
Cares for her meat but not her soul.
Looks through windows and falls down holes,
And how I feel sorry for those baby moles.

My cat is ferocious,
Just like a lion,
Her amber eyes can be raging with fire,
Just like burning tyres!

The greatest lion of them all,
The ruler of the animal kingdom.
She also thinks she's the Queen of Sheba
And all I have to do is feed her.

My cat is ferocious,
Just like a lion,
Beware all you people,
If you want to buy her!

Daniel Dawson-Brown (11)
The Shrubbery School

My First Day At School

First day at school
I was very nervous
The day went fast
But in PE I was last.

Second day of school
The teacher bawls
'You're late again
And now you little fool, you've forgot your pen.'

Third day of school
Got some new friends
But can never play 'cause school never ends.

Fourth day of school
On time at last
I wondered if we would have to study the past.

Fifth day of school
The weekend in sight
And at last I'll be able to stay up at night.

Helena Sheldrake (10)
The Shrubbery School

The Volcano

The volcano against the clouds stands high,
Its shadow covering the whole of the town's space,
Hiding the wondrous blue of the sky,
We are forced to look at its threatening face.

Its bubbling lava gets hotter each day,
Then one day it starts to overflow,
And burns everything in its way,
Then the molten ashes begin to glow.

All it covers it will destroy,
All the worries, all the fears,
When it's over it causes joy,
We hope it won't happen
For many years.

Niamh Jordan (11)
The Shrubbery School

MY FAMILY

My mum, my dad, my sister and brother
Have different characters from each other.

For instance, my dad would shout
'Up to bed right now, right now.
'Cause otherwise we will have a row.'
And as for my mum, you don't want to know,
She always shouts at me, now you know.
My brother is a little pest,
One day he even pinched my vest.
My little sister, she is worst of all,
She slapped me right against the wall.
She punched me in my belly she did, then she said I was a twit.
I said she was one and she had a fit.
I got the blame, I might have known,
Got sent to my bedroom all on my own.
I ate all the chocolate in my room
And that made me full of gloom.
So I made up a dance to Vengaboys
And lay in bed with all my toys.

I love them and hate them in one go
Now that is my family, now you know
So toodle-loo off you go.

Harriet Pallister (9)
The Shrubbery School

Jaguar

The jaguar
Is smooth, sleek -
Just like the car.
It run as fast as light
And seems to kill and eat
Without a fight.

It is feared
Throughout the world
Not just by the deer.
It climbs the trees,
Never caught,
'Cause the poacher always flees.

With its soft, padded feet
It creeps under the tall canopy
Waiting for the prey it will eat.
'The jaguar should never be seen
It is great . . . but don't touch it,
You don't know where it's been!'

Sam Wager (11)
The Shrubbery School

You Always Scare Me Brother

Every time I come home for tea,
You make me *jump* and shout at me,
You look like the spirit of the night,
I never liked you from my first sight!

Your hair looks like fire with flames so red-hot,
Your face is as round as a pot,
Your clothes give me the shivers from head to toe,
Your voice gives me the fright as it's so low.

You always scare me,
I have to say,
And now you will have to pay!
For what you've done,
You'll have to run,
So hurry up and be gone!

Saffia Ahmed (10)
The Shrubbery School

My Friends

My friend's hair is the colour of chocolate ice cream,
Her hair is as smooth as her dreams,
She is as happy as a flower,
And she has lots of power,
Her name is Sara.

My friend's hair is like spaghetti,
Her face is as pale as whipped cream,
Her cheeks are pink as jelly,
And she is light as a feather,
Her name is Hannah.

My friend's hair is like dozens and dozens of flowers in fields,
Her favourite food is pizza,
Her face is as round as roses,
Her zodiac is a snake,
Her name is Jessica.

My teacher's hair is a mixture of colours,
Her red hair stands out to be strong and powerful,
Her cheeks are as rosy as pink,
Smiles and hugs that's what she brings,
Her name is Mrs Williams.

Kelly Ing (10)
The Shrubbery School

BIRTHDAYS

When you get out of your bed,
You rush ahead,
Go downstairs,
Open your presents,
Tear open your cards,
Dress in your best outfit and wait!
Ding, dong,
Happy birthday!
Shout relations and friends,
Then the song starts,
Then we all eat party food,
Sausages, cakes until we're full,
Drink lemonade, it's really cool,
I cut the cake with a scarlet ribbon on it,
Pass it round,
So everyone gets a bit,
Wow! More presents and cards,
A new texter, and a new pair of high heels,
Make-up and a book on girls in glamour,
All the relations go away,
I'm on my own, left to play.

Bavane Sivayogaiswaran (8)
The Shrubbery School

RAINBOW COLOURS

My sad rainbow colours
Red scars from a beaten up child, hot coal, volcano just erupted.
Orange the colour of a fierce tiger, the colour of a cigarette just lit.
Yellow the colour of a bruise just healing up.
Green the colour of a bruise just healing up.
Blue the colour of a shivering cold body.
Indigo the colour of dried up blood on your leg.
Violet the colour of a newborn baby that's ill and cold.

My happy rainbow colours
Red ripe rosy strawberries.
Orange juice quenching my thirst.
Yellow glistening glimmering sun.
Green grass shines on the hills.
Blue berry ice cream melts in my mouth.
Indigo plums picked in a basket.
Violet flowers cover the field.

Colours make a rainbow of joy!

Alice Davis (11)
The Shrubbery School

Animals

Big animals, little animals,
Elephants and mice,
Long animals, short animals,
Snakes and ants,
Fat animals, thin animals,
Hippopotamus and lizards,
Tall animals, short animals,
Giraffes and bugs,
Mammals and camels,
Birds and snails,
Fish with tails,
Fluffy and furry,
Silky and smooth,
Slippy and slimy,
Rough and tough,
Some eat meat,
Some eat greens,
They are amazing,
In everything!

Charlie Briscoe (8)
The Shrubbery School

CAVES

Caves are long, wide
And very dark inside
They have sharp teeth with a huge mouth
Who knows what's inside
At night they speak
Wind roars out of their huge mouths and in again.

At daytime they sleep on their front
Quiet as a mouse
All the darkness has gone
They do not speak, not a sound
As they sleep on their front with their mouths closed.

Night falls and the cave is awake
They are speaking to each other in the darkness
With their huge mouths and their jaws like a shark
No one knows what's inside
Caves are long and wide and very dark inside.

Luke Aminu (8)
The Shrubbery School

CHARLIE

Charlie jumps up and squeals.
He has eyes that are as big as wheels.
Charlie's fur's like a penguin.
His eyes are as happy as a boy getting what he wants.
His tail is like a spring morning flower,
Swaying in the wind.
His paws are as soft as pillows.
Charlie is my favourite dog.

Jessica Rainbow (11)
The Shrubbery School

New York

Monday. Fly into JFK,
Jet lag pulling me down; 8 o'clock at night.
Get a yellow cab, to a grand skyscraper residence.
Wow! It's like a dazzling star . . . the hotel.

The next day, Tuesday.
Shopping on 5th Avenue, then fun and games.
Play on Wall Street, lose a million dollars.
Totally depressed. Take the subway . . . back to the hotel.

Wednesday, never going to the 'Wall' again!
Nearly broke. Cheap tickets on Times Square for Broadway.
A musical . . . Cats. Purrfect! Can't afford a cab.
Walk through midnight crowds . . . back to the hotel.

Thursday. Off to the Empire State Building,
Although I am scared of heights.
At the top . . . and just look at the drop!
'Aah!' I scream in fright,
Dodge along the sidewalks . . . then back to the hotel!

Friday, extremely cold. Ice skating in Central Park.
Next, the Statue of Liberty. Towering over the harbour,
Looking like a monster woman, with a snow crown.
Decide not to go to the top. Remember yesterday?
Through the graffiti subway in China Town . . . back to the hotel.

Later fly out of JFK,
Leaving the Big Apple behind for rainy London.
Not too bad.
For it's Saturday . . . back to the football!

William Viles (10)
The Shrubbery School

DADS

You can get fat dads,
Thin dads,
Scented dads,
Rented dads,
Working dads,
Lurking dads,
Joking dads,
Croaking dads.

Dads that learn,
Dads that burn trees,
Dads with knobbly knees,
Dads that sail over stormy seas,
Dads that abseil,
Dads that give people mail,
Dads that go to the January sale.

You can get all sorts of dads,
Mad dads,
Sad dads,
Rich dads,
Poor dads,
Itchy dads,
Door fixer dads,
Buzzing dads,
Guzzling dads,
Snoozing dads,
Cruising dads.

Dads are lovely,
Dads have a mind,
Dads are one of a kind.

Jasmine Adkins (8)
The Shrubbery School

My Life

When I get up in the morning,
I start yawning.
I hope for a cup of tea
And pancakes waiting for me.

When I am sad and need a cuddle
Mum will be there on the double.
Then I take the dog for a walk,
I see my friend, we have a talk.

Bella, Majella and Rose-Mary
Are playing a game without me.
As I go into the playground,
You wouldn't say there's not a sound.

Today we've got art,
I need to paint a horse and cart.
Hooray! School is over!
Home to my dog Rover.

Home from school,
Tea is ready.
Do homework, watch telly,
Then Mum says, 'Go to beddy.'

I go to bed,
Stare at the moon,
Have a great dream,
But I'm still in my room.

Here I am, it's tomorrow,
Another day full of sorrow.
Games to play, work to do,
Just another day.

Ciara McMahon (8)
The Shrubbery School

Me And My Sister Always Argue!

Me and my sister always argue,
I don't know a time when we haven't!
Every day I come home,
There she goes fighting with me!
She kicks me on the leg,
She punches me in the tummy.

One day I asked her,
'Shall we be friends?'
'You are joking,' she said,
'I will never be mates with you!'

Another day I would watch TV
And she would be in her room,
'Ow, ow,' she would say,
'Stop punching me, stop kicking me,'
My sister would hurt herself
And say I did it!

Mom comes upstairs,
Straight into my room, smacks me,
Goes into my sister's room,
Asks her 'You are alright?'
My sister would say,
'Just look at my arms and legs,'
Mom comes into my room,
'You are grounded,' she would say,
'Now go into your sister's room and say you're sorry,'
I go into her room and say 'Sorry for nothing.'

Lana Mohammed (8)
The Shrubbery School

YOUR SISTER

Your sister might be awful
Your sister might call you names
Your sister might be kind, some day
And let you win all the games.

Your mum might tell your sister off
You might stick up for her
Even though she might be nasty
You'll always love her.

Your sister might be the worst sister in the world
But she thinks that she's the best
If she gets on your nerves
Then you should call her pest.

Me and my sister fight a lot
But we get along quite often
Sometimes she helps me with my homework
And I thank her a lot.

Sometimes my sister lets me stroke her cat
And lets me play with her toys
But I don't think it's fair that she gets
The good looking boys.

Maybe I should say sorry
For the things I've done to her
But sometimes I think she should say sorry
Because she started it first.

Katie Richards (8)
The Shrubbery School

FOOTBALL MATCH

Coming out of the tunnel
The crowd are screaming mad
Baying for a win
For the glory they had
Shaking like a jelly
With excitement in my belly.

I run through
Look at the linesman
No offside
I thought it went in
But it went wide.

I keep going
Covering all the pitch
To score a goal
Would make me feel rich.

Oh my God
I have just had a near miss
I never give up
I am thinking about the Cup.

I kick the ball in the net
Goal disallowed
I am so angry
I want to kick the crowd.

The whistle blows
The crowd are sad
We lost the game.

Drew Huggins (11)
The Shrubbery School

Horrid School

In a school, far beyond;
A grey mist clears the way.
In the school when teachers laugh
Children cry,
The dinners are like snails and worms,
It makes my stomach churn and whirl.

In a school, far beyond;
The bullies are crocodiles,
Nobody for miles.
The teacher stands there
In the mist,
She's a witch!

In a school, far beyond;
The teachers don't teach.
They leave the children
In a room,
No food or drink in sight,
Most go red, the rest just die.

In a school, far beyond;
The teachers are like monsters.
They creak and crack,
Their bones are like skeletons,
Their teeth are like sharks,
They eat everything,
Nothing lasts.

Jordan Woodley (8)
The Shrubbery School

SPORTS DAY

I woke up this morning
With a dreadful thought
That awful day is here
My school call it sports day
I just call it fear.

It's not the ice cream man that comes
Or the sweets or drinks
But I know the three-legged race
Would have me in a jinx.

It has me paired with Grace you see
A joyful girl in class
But when it comes to sports day
She goes a little mad.

I have to run 80 meters flat
With Grace tied to my leg
She is six foot three
Shaped like an egg
A giant next to me.

That's the problem, can you see?
We'll finish last again
It happens every year
To Grace and little me.

Joshua Hannon (11)
The Shrubbery School

I Hate Scissors

I hate scissors.

H orrible little scissors,
A ngry people use them,
T o hurt, to cut people,
E veryone can get hurt by horrible little scissors.

S illy little scissors,
C an hurt a lot,
I magine everyone used
S cissors to hurt, if people are
S arcastic, swear
O r
R aving mad,
S cissors will get into it and that makes me *sad!*

Sara Momen (10)
The Shrubbery School

On The Way To Ten

One, curly hair over a fat little body,
Two, words start coming out of my mouth,
Three, I go on my first trip abroad to France,
Four, rode my bike without any stabilisers,
Five, swimming without anything,
Six, going to my first theme park (Alton Towers),
Seven, I go on my first trip in an aeroplane to Canada,
Eight, I entered my first running event and won it,
Nine, I won the league in rugby,
Ten, I entered my first cross country event.

Ross McDonald (10)
Town Junior School

War

War was declared,
We heard it all.
Silence had broken,
In the autumn fall.

Hitler had done it,
He crossed the line.
The invasion of Poland,
He gave us the sign.

Crying old relatives,
They'd seen it before.
'Not again,' she sobbed,
Her tears said war.

Now it was time,
To get away,
From war to the country,
That's what they say.

The young and old,
From under thirty,
Went to war
Bold and dirty.

At night it was dark,
Not a light to be seen.
Harder for Hitler,
And his light beam.

At war they built,
Their muddy trenches.
The siren sounds,
Clear the parks and benches.

Now it's all over,
Hip, hip, hooray.
And that was the end,
Of Hitler's day.

Eliott Rhodes (11)
Town Junior School

The Soldier

On a dark night the soldier lay on a muddy bed,
For company his gun and bullets of lead,
Awaiting the sound of an exploding shell,
For friend or foe no one can tell.

The first morning sun, the soldier awakes,
And picks up his gun for England's sake,
He strides to his post,
And thinks of his family, his mother the most.

It was afternoon when the order came,
That was to end the soldier's reign,
He took the order like any soldier did,
And did his captain's dangerous bid.

The soldier crept into the enemy camp,
The weather murky and damp,
Suddenly though the officer heard his sound,
And shot, the soldier fell to the ground.

His wife and children shed a tear,
For someone who they held so dear,
But the soldier lay on his muddy bed,
For company his gun and bullets of lead.

Katherine Daniels (10)
Town Junior School

Why Do Bombers Have To Bomb?

Why do bombers have to bomb?
Bomb our country one by one,
Children crying very loud,
Hoping bombers will calm it down.

Why do bombers have to bomb?
Bomb our country one by one,
Soldiers dying in the war,
Parents crying more and more.

Why do bombers have to bomb?
Bomb our country one by one,
ARP warden telling you off,
For leaving an inch of light about.

Why do bombers have to bomb?
Bomb our country one by one.

Brittany Campbell (10)
Town Junior School

Pollution Personified

She comes spilling out of chimneys,
Comes pounding down the town,
Spilling litter, dodging dustbins,
Leaving poisonous powders all over the ground.

As she soars above the filth she has scattered haphazardly,
Mammals run and hide, not knowing she will find,
Stretching out her bony fingers, reaching for the mammal's neck,
Squeezing tightly until the mammals hold no life left.

She rampages through beauty without a care,
Leaving damage and destruction everywhere,
Breathing poison, spreading acid,
Killing wildlife with plant survival very rare.

Well I think she has done enough damage for one day,
But she will be back, I can assure you of that,
Of course she is pollution the predator,
While nature is the prey.

Samuel Clarke (11)
Town Junior School

WAR AT WAR

World War I
Has gone,
World War II
Has begun.
Can't be as bad,
Just as sad,
People fight
For our right
With all their might.

World War I
Has gone,
World War II
Has begun.
People crying,
People dying,
I'm so glad it's over.

Tania Riley (11)
Town Junior School

WAR

War is ever so bad,
War is making people sad.
War is making people die,
War is making people cry.
War is like a wolf in the night,
And lots of people are going to fight.
War was started when Hitler spoke,
But people took it for a joke.
Germans are in the air flying,
And it leads to people dying.
People are making aircrafts and they are skilled,
But lots of them are getting killed.
Lots of people are sad,
And lots of kids have lost their dads!

Joshua Holmes (11)
Town Junior School

WORLD WAR II

War tears through lives,
Like an unmerciful hurricane,
Destroying hopes and dreams,
Causing nothing but pain,
War is full of people dying,
War is full of families crying,
Bombs are dropping everywhere,
Hitler destroys without a care.

Peace is what Britain wants,
It's nice to have it around,
Peace is kind not like war,
Peace is quiet and silent.

Josie Perry (10)
Town Junior School

War

War began when Hitler spoke,
Everyone thought it was just a joke.
Armies took over lots of places,
Blood on bodies, blood on faces.
On steam trains lots of little children went,
Even if they did not want to be sent.
People screamed and cried all night,
Because they were scared and full of fright.
We hope that this is just a nightmare,
Because this war we cannot bare.
We have left our family and our home,
We have no one left, nothing to own.

I never feel happy, just sad,
Now I know this world is bad.
People staring,
Fires a-blaring.
I can't wait until the war comes to a halt,
This is all Hitler's fault.

Stefanie Cunningham (11)
Town Junior School

Faces

Some people have blonde hair,
Some people have brown,
Some people have beards that grow down and down,
Some people have brown eyes,
Some people have blue,
But whatever your face looks like,
I'll still like you!

Natalie Millard (8)
Town Junior School

War Vs Peace

War brings peril,
War brings fear,
It penetrates
Like a thrusting spear.
It drowns the world
In its bloody pool,
Germany is evil under Hitler's rule.

Peace brings joy,
Peace brings pleasure,
Loving, warm and soft
As a feather.
It moves the world one step closer,
To perfect harmony.

John Daniels (10)
Town Junior School

World At War

The world is being blown to pieces,
There's people dying,
Their friends and family are crying.
I want the world to stop the war,
The world is full of sad faces,
People saying they will come back,
But in fact they are dying.
Families splitting up one by one,
Their moms and dads living for
The world is breaking up,
The world is meant to help each other,
Not killing because of beliefs.

Mark Collins (10)
Town Junior School

WAR AND PEACE

War and peace are not the same,
War doesn't have any fame.
Peace is beautiful, peace isn't bad,
But war is always very sad.
People get shot,
Peace is good and war is not.
Germans are invading our town,
All civilians do is frown.
Soldiers are getting hurt more and more,
As they are sent out to war.
Why did this war start?
Why did it tear us apart?

Thomas Nicholas (10)
Town Junior School

TIME

The river runs by to meet the sea,
Can't stop at all, no time you see.
The tide rushes in and then runs away,
'Are we late?' it asks, no one wanted to say.

The trees in the woods stand together like one,
But leaves are brushed by the wind and are gone,
Then there's the sun with all its might,
Rushing to the leaves before it's night,
Who says 'You mustn't be late!'
It's the clock of course and that's often late.

Laura Graham (9)
Town Junior School

Pollution

It charges around on our earth,
Destroying plants with its vile stench,
Leaving a long, black, staining trail,
It belches out trails of choking smog.

Innocent animals suffer,
As it strangles and suffocates them,
It traps fish with its oily grip,
It coats birds in black sludge.

The ozone layer is its punch bag,
It hurls its javelins of acid rain,
Its discus makes an arc of litter,
It races to mankind's destruction.

Ben Kerr (11)
Town Junior School

Pollution

He rampages through the woods,
Leaving a shadow of destruction.

He poisons rivers with gases,
That come out of cans and bottles and glasses.

He tips over dustbins and throws cans everywhere,
He destroys fields to make factories that belch out smoke and
poison into the air.

Acid rain breaks buildings down,
And makes plants crumble to the ground.

You may not think pollution is there
But he is . . . he is *everywhere!*

Thomas Smith (10)
Town Junior School

Christmas

Leaves are falling
The trees are bare,
Mothers are calling,
'Put this hat over your hair!'

It was Christmas Day
And I wanted to play
But Mom said, 'No,
There's too much snow.'

It was time for dinner,
The candles were lit,
I could have sworn Mom was thinner
By a tiny bit.

Anthony Williams (10)
Town Junior School

War And Peace

Looking back in time, at that awful war,
I seem to never see what people did it for.
It did nothing good, but only bad,
It hurts to see how many people were sad.
Why did they do it? I'll never know,
It went on for five years, even in the snow.
England really never won,
How many people were expected to live? None.
The Germans tried to kill us all,
All of us little or tall.
I hope that the world will learn, even the poor,
Never to take part in a war.

Sarah Coxall (10)
Town Junior School

Bombed

The giant craft overhead at night,
Filled with soldiers prepared to fight,
Dark shadows flying way up high,
Round black bombs fill the sky,
Loud whooshes from the aeroplanes,
Dropping bombs with careful aim,
Quickly to the Anderson Shelter,
It's like a ride on a helter skelter,
An adventure for me because I'm small,
Looking at Mother standing proud and tall,
Proud of Father fighting for freedom,
Proud of her children although without reason,
War prowls bloodthirsty around every corner,
Destroying the 'pie' like little Jack Horner,
Oh no, another explosion!
That German will get a promotion,
The night air is cold with war,
Now our house is a house no more,
But a pile of rubble, all is lost,
All our belongings destroyed at a cost,
Now we've been bombed and made homeless,
We pull together so we're not so hopeless.

Megan Morrall (11)
Town Junior School

The Cold

Noses are red
Feet are blue
I've got a cold
Now I've given it to you!

Amy Scott (8)
Town Junior School

Behind The Enemy Lines

Huge explosions down below
Fire the colour of crimson wine,
The Germans look up, high above
They see a plane just like a dove.

I scan the area
There I see
A factory, working?
Wow, whoopee!

Clouds creamy white
The skies clear blue,
The plane soars high
Down below the Germans sigh.

Suddenly, all in a flash
My allies pass over me,

The bullets are fired
The bombs are dropped,

By then I know my job is done.

Paul Lee (10)
Town Junior School

Pencils

Pencils are sharp,
Pencils are blunt.
Pencils have legs so
You have to hunt.
Pencils, pencils,
Pencils, what are
Pencils?

Georgina Horrell (8)
Town Junior School

The War

War was declared,
Then it began,
People scattered,
At the sound of a gun.

The sky lit up,
When a bomb was dropped,
When a bomb was dropped,
The sky lit up.

The children were gone,
Their mothers upset,
The house was all empty,
Tears down cheeks, all wet.

The sky lit up,
When a bomb was dropped,
When a bomb was dropped,
The sky lit up.

The air was dirty,
The air was dusty,
The air was dull,
The air was musty.

War was upon us!

Jenny Green (11)
Town Junior School

World War II

War has an evil look in its eye,
Because of Hitler,
The people sigh,
Because of the cruelty and mess,
We kiss our children God bless.

With all the bombs being dropped,
Lots of poor people's ears are going to pop,
Old bad memories from the old folk,
They whine, stop, please stop,
This is World War II.

Christopher Wright (10)
Town Junior School

THE CAT

Clever little cat,
Running up hill,
It kept on going,
Only until,
It smelt a slice of chicken,
Just down the road,
In a cottage on the left,
With its own door code.
It went in the cat flap
And saw some chicken on the shelf,
It jumped up there and took a peep,
And said to himself,
'Clever old Grandma,
Left out some dinner for me.
And oh what a surprise she did have
When I took it home for tea.'
But Granny came in
From shopping in the town,
And shooed the cat outside
With a very horrible frown.
And silly little pussy
Thinking he would win,
But then he went down the road,
And got a double gin!

Helen Page (8)
Town Junior School

Pollution

He rampages through the air,
Destroying everything in sight.
In smoky shadow by day,
And poisonous air by night.

Whatever plant he looks at
Will die.
His power is like the
Fiery eyes of Medusa.

Upon earth where he lies,
Weaving a deadly plot.

We must make him stop,
Only about ten years from now
There will be nothing left.

With his massive cape,
Of destruction, he covers the world.

It is *pollution!*

Benjamin Godwin (11)
Town Junior School

I Was Evacuated!

I was evacuated to a place
Which was called
A countryside, a farmyard
Little Weirworld.

I lived with a man
Who helped me a lot
He was kind and generous
And called Mr Tom.

He read me stories
And played games too
But I had a wish
And one day it came true.

Anyway, Mom wanted me back
And that's where I stayed
Till Mr Tom came and saved
My little heart.

Naomi Parton-Smith (11)
Town Junior School

War Poem!

We're at war,
Everyone knows,
Hitler's made no friends,
But foes.

Bombs on top of roofs,
Scattered all over the place,
Children had an unhappy face
As they saw their houses turned
To smithereens.

The siren sounds,
Now into the shelter,
Everyone screaming,
'Help! Help! Aaahhh!'

Sounds, shots, cries from everywhere,
The war is declared!
The war is declared!

Rachael Evans (10)
Town Junior School

DOLPHINS

Dolphins in the sea,
Dolphins, dolphins,
Swishing, swashing,
Splashing, sploshing,
Dolphins in the sea.

Dolphins in the sea
Dolphins, dolphins,
Playing, swaying,
Jumping, spraying,
Dolphins in the sea.

Dolphins in the sea,
Dolphins, dolphins,
Squeaking, squawking,
Chattering, talking,
Dolphins in the sea.

Joshua Millwood (9)
Town Junior School

HITLER

War had broken out
Hitler had done it
And it made Granny pout
Mom nearly had a fit

He'd taken over Poland
He's just crossed the line
Hitler's had his ships manned
He's already given the sign

We'd warned him once
Notice he took not
For he's just stamped over France
I guess he forgot

We had one damn good army
When he realised he said, 'Blimey!
They're gonna kick my Heinie!'
He shot his head, so we had VE.

Mitchell Griffiths (11)
Town Junior School

WAR POEM!

For a moment Britain was silent,
It was extremely violent
German bombers dropping bombs everywhere,
People were scared.

People panicking on the ground,
The horrid sounds
Then Britain won,
And dropping their guns.

Everyone screaming and shouting
For dear life,
The shelter so cold as ice,
People sighing
When people are crying.

Sam Simmonds (10)
Town Junior School

POLLUTION

The pollution is spilling,
His poisonous gases,
The pollution is killing,
The trees and grasses.

Destruction is his middle name,
Devastation is his fame,
Killing is what he aimed,
So he should feel ashamed.

What can we do?
That person is who?
It could be a disaster,
But we've got to stop that monster!

William Fitzpatrick (11)
Town Junior School

POLLUTION

People dropping litter everywhere,
It looks like no one cares,
The bins are empty,
But the streets are full.

Factories flaming all the time,
How can we stop this terrible crime?
Gas steam flying in the blackened air,
I don't know why nobody's scared.

Pollution taking over the sky,
Why can't we stop it? Why? Why? Why?
We can't let the litters win,
So let's finally use the bin.

Josh Robinson & Rory Stretton
Town Junior School

SCHOOL

I woke up early and I was tired,
I scrambled out of bed,
knowing today was the day
I started to sweat and feel the dread.

It began at 9am,
the dreaded school.
We all pushed
our way through the door.

The first lesson was maths
my favourite of them all.
I was concentrating hard,
while others began to get bored.

Break was great,
as it was our football.
I played brilliantly,
scoring twice in a two-two draw.

The next lesson was English,
the one I found hardest.
So I tried hard, but others didn't try,
especially the smartest.

After lunch was double computer lesson,
which was brill.
We even got to try the internet,
which gave us a thrill.

Thomas Clarke (8)
Town Junior School

THE TRAIN

As I step on the train
I see mothers crying in shame,
We all wave our mothers goodbye
All they could do was cry and cry,
They shout goodbye to their mothers
Blowing kisses like all the others,
The train began to chug and chug
Boys and girls start to hug,
The train disappears into the mist
Soldiers shouting with clenched fists.

Charlotte Vernon (11)
Town Junior School

WHAT IS YOUR WISH?

I wish my little sister was big
I could play older games with her.
I wish I was a footballer
I would become famous with money.
I wish I was a millionaire
I could buy anything in the world.
I wish I owned 65 limousines
I could arrive looking cool.
I wish I knew everything in the world
Then everyone would be jealous.
I wish I had five gold rings,
I look cool with the limousines.
I wish I was a witch that just had to point for magic
I could have anything in the world.
I wish I was top in all subjects
I would get all As in them.

Jason Dhaliwal (8)
Wylde Green College

What Is Your Wish?

I wish I had a jet-ski on wheels
I could get to school on time.
I wish I could be eighteen
I could marry my girlfriend.
I wish I could be a big apple
I could explore an animal's body.
I wish I could live forever
I could see new inventions.
I wish me and my friend went to Spain
Thomas could see my new house.
I wish Daniel could come to my house
He could play on my Land Rover.
I wish I could be the teacher
I could tell everybody to play.
I wish I had all the Neo cards
I could be the master of cards.
I wish I could be a snowman
I would be in the snow.

Richard Sheen (7)
Wylde Green College

What's Your Wish?

I wish I was very rich so I could give money to the poor.
I wish I could be a doctor to help the sick people more.

I wish my baby cousin Shana was older and could come and play,
We could watch scary movies together every day.

I wish I had a toy shop and I would play there every day,
I wish I could go to the Bahamas and swim with dolphins
and watch them play.

Ebony Hare
Wylde Green College

James' Wishes

I wish I could fly
Up in the sky so high,
I would watch the birds fly by,
And I watch the sun go down in the sky.

I wish I was a footballer,
How happy I would be,
Scoring goals for all my team,
And getting excited, I am glad
I play for Manchester United.

I wish the sun would shine every day,
So my sister and I could go out to play,
And all this rain would go away,
And come again another day.

I wish all the sick could be well,
The hungry could have food,
The lonely could have some friends,
This would put me in a good mood.

James Massey (7)
Wylde Green College

I Am The King Of The Universe

I am the king of the universe, wicked at maths
Cool at English and the best at geography
I am clever, dashing and so handsome
That all the girls start chasing me.

I am the king of the universe, I like showing off
Like being spiteful, proud or boastful
I have an answer to everything you say
But my mum says I am still delightful.

I am the king of the universe, an expert
At history, but why I am so brilliant is a mystery
I walk down the street and everyone bows at my feet
You will never meet anyone better than me.

Alastair Day (9)
Wylde Green College

CHOCOLATE

Chocolate is a dream,
It is especially delicious with cream.
All sorts of fillings to taste,
Strawberry, toffee made to a paste,
And many more flavours to tempt your buds,
If you ate them all you would dribble with suds

There are boxes and bars,
Lollies and jars.
All shapes and sizes,
Also drinks and ices.
Eggs, buttons, biscuits and cakes,
There's no end to what you can make.

Sometimes the taste is soft and creamy,
Sometimes the taste is hard and crunchy,
Occasionally there's nuts and sultanas,
Some even taste of bananas.

Some people are addicted,
They just can't refuse it.
They end up overweight,
And just can't lose it.

James Casserley (10)
Wylde Green College

What Is Your Wish?

I wish I had a real PlayStation
With every game you can get.
I wish I had a pony
I could go galloping over the field.
I wish I had all the house points
So nobody could catch up with me.
I wish I had the nicest dress
So everybody would be jealous.
I wish I could fly
So that I could get to places quicker.
I wish that I was magic
So that I could walk through walls.
I wish I was a princess
Because I could live in a castle.
I wish that Lisa out of Steps
Could come to my house to have a disco.

Lucy Barber (7)
Wylde Green College

Cheese, The Food From Hell

This fattening, squirmy, slidy snack,
If you leave it, it will turn black . . .
Not much of a treat,
It smells like someone's feet.
Cheese is like manky mud that you find in an old shoe,
Smelly like a pig sty.
You would find it up your nose,
It's radioactive and it glows.
Cheese is liked by Wallace and Gromit,
But when I taste it, I want to vomit.

Andrew Warr (9)
Wylde Green College

WHAT IS YOUR WISH?

I wish I had a shire horse
I could gallop everywhere.
I wish I had two trees
That grew sweets and gold.
I wish my mum and dad had better legs
They could go riding on a bike.
I wish I could have all the toys I wanted
To keep me going and so I don't get bored.
I wish I could go to the Caribbean with my family
So I could get a suntan.
I wish I had a flying saucer
I could go anywhere I wanted.
I wish that Sclub7 could come to my house
I could have a disco.

Ian Murdoch (8)
Wylde Green College

WHAT IS YOUR WISH?

I wish that I had a rabbit
I could stroke her, it would be nice.
I wish I went in a sports car with Lucy
I could go to the beach with her.
I wish I could take my mum and dad to school
I could hug them while I did my work.
I wish that I had a posh dress
Everyone would fancy me.
I wish that Gold House would lose
Then Green House would be better at sport.
I wish that my dad had a flying car
Then I could get over the traffic and get to school very early.

Francesca Marks (8)
Wylde Green College

Chocolate Concrete

On Monday morning I run into school,
Sometimes I feel a bit of a fool.
I look at the menu for my favourite sweet
I hope it is chocolate concrete, a special treat.

It's delicious and tasty and rich chocolate brown,
If it's not the concrete there would be a frown.
It's hard as real concrete but melts in your mouth,
If it's not on the menu I think I would move south.
It's crunchy, yummy and ever so sweet,
All other puddings can it beat.

I love it with custard, chocolate sauce or ice cream
Chocolate concrete is really such a dream.
I hope I have seconds and possible thirds,
Even if I have to eat Mr Bird's.

Max Fitzgerald-Owen (9)
Wylde Green College

What Is Your Wish?

I wish I was a ghost
I could scare people when they are asleep.
I wish I was a football player
I could kick the ball at people and foul them.
I wish I had a flying motorbike
I could fly over traffic jams.
I wish I could punch people to other countries
If they tried to hurt me.
I wish I had super power
To hug my mum and dad really hard.

Tom Acton (7)
Wylde Green College

THE CHOCOLATE POEM

When I eat chocolate
Caramel comes out like red blood,
Cool, beautiful, it looks like
I am in a different world,
Sweet as toffee.

When the taste comes out
I never let go of it
And never say no to chocolate.

I love chocolate, I can eat
A whole packet of chocolate,
It's fantastic, it's cool as ice
And as cool as me.

Syra Ahmad (9)
Wylde Green College

WHAT IS YOUR WISH?

I wish I was a scientist
I could discover new diseases.
I wish I had a sweetie house
I could eat sweets all the time.
I wish I won a million pounds
I could be on television like Judith Keppel.
I wish I was a flower fairy
I could bring joy to everybody.
I wish I was everybody's friend
I could play with everyone.
I wish I was teacher's pet
I could do anything.

Lauren Ross (8)
Wylde Green College

WHAT IS YOUR WISH?

I wish I went to Florida
Because I could swim in the pool.
I wish I was strong
So I could help people.
I wish I was rich
So I could give money to the poor.
I wish I had a car
So I could take people where they need to go.
I wish I had a rabbit
Because I like to feed them.
I wish I had a cat
So I could train it.

Karandeep Virdee (7)
Wylde Green College

I WISH

I wish I was a dinosaur
I could squish things.
I wish I had a motorbike
I could get home quicker.
I wish I was a football
I could get kicked around.
I wish I could marry Lucy
I could have babies.
I wish playtime was on all day
I wouldn't have to do work.
I wish I was invincible
I would never die.

Sam Reece (7)
Wylde Green College

WHAT IS YOUR WISH?

I wish I was an astronaut
So I could float about in space.
I wish I had a car which could fly
So I could drive in the air.
I wish I was an artist
So I could draw animals.
I wish I got into the gala
And got first place.
I wish I was a footballer
So I could get lots of money.

David Morris (7)
Wylde Green College